BLACKPOOL TOWER
A HISTORY

BLACKPOOL TOWER
A HISTORY

Peter Walton

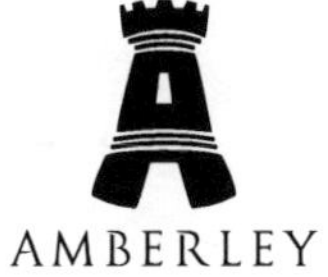

In writing this history I have been repeatedly impressed and even awed by the sheer determination and tenacity of Sir John Bickerstaffe, who with great effort carried through an idea which on the surface appeared to be fanciful, ludicrous, even foolhardy.

Bill Curtis, *Blackpool Tower*, 1988

First published 2016

Amberley Publishing
The Hill, Stroud
Gloucestershire, GL5 4EP

www.amberley-books.com

Copyright © Peter Walton, 2016

The right of Peter Walton to be identified as the Author of this work has been asserted in accordance with the Copyrights, Designs and Patents Act 1988.

ISBN 978 1 4456 4498 1 (print)
ISBN 978 1 4456 4518 6 (ebook)

British Library Cataloguing in Publication Data.
A catalogue record for this book is available from the British Library.

Typesetting and Origination by Amberley Publishing
Printed in the UK.

CONTENTS

PREFACE

This book is a story of management, finance and strategy. While it is about show business, it is first and foremost about the bricks and mortar of show business, not the stars or the music. In many ways the Blackpool Tower Co. is an example of Victorian entrepreneurship, and shows how a challenging commercial idea was turned into a concrete reality primarily through the determination and management skills of a single person. Many of the problems encountered and the ideas used to solve them have their counterpart in the modern economy. The life cycle of the Blackpool Tower Co. is also a good example of a model company life cycle. Of course the legal, ethical and governance framework today is different, and the light tax structure that enabled people who made fortunes to keep them and invest again, is also a thing of the past.

ACKNOWLEDGEMENT OF COPYRIGHT

The author and publisher would like to thank the following people and organisations for permission to use copyright material in this book.

The cover photograph is from the Blackpool Local and Family History Centre. The drawing of the Douglas Tower is by kind permission of Manx National Heritage. The photograph 'The Tower, the town and the seafront, Blackpool, from the south-west, 1934' is the copyright of Historic England and the licensor is canmore.org.uk. The photographs of the Bickerstaffe family monument are by Tony Sharkey. The photograph of Bernard Delfont on holiday is the copyright of Sue Delfont, to whom we are grateful for its use. The 1969 photograph of Billy Marsh, Bernard Delfont, Michael Grade, Leslie Grade and Dennis van Thal has been licensed by Trinity Mirror/Mirrorpix/Alamy. All other photographs have been licensed by the Blackpool Local and Family History Centre.

Every attempt has been made to seek permission for copyright material used in this book. However, if we have inadvertently used copyright material without permission/acknowledgement we apologise and we will make the necessary correction at the first opportunity.

ACKNOWLEDGEMENTS

I owe a great debt to four stalwarts of Blackpool history: Tony Sharkey (head of local history at Blackpool Central Library) has been central to the project, giving me access to the local history collection, especially newspaper archives, and extensive photographs, and encouragement with the project; Barry Band (veteran Blackpool journalist, publisher and historian) has also been generous with his time and knowledge, especially his detailed first-hand experience; Ted Lightbown (Blackpool historian and archivist) helped with background briefing and gave significant help with checking accuracy; and Ann Lightbown (archivist at the Blackpool Tower Archive) who presides over precious original material from the Tower Co. and made available the Tower company's yearbooks. They all have given generously their time and knowledge and also provided access to precious primary material. Without their goodwill and active collaboration this book would not have been possible.

One of the pleasures of historical research is in fact that the researcher is often the recipient of the 'kindness of strangers' in the form of enthusiastic help from many people who look after repositories of information and who are enthused by individual searches for information. In this way I am grateful to Manx National Heritage, Companies House, the British Library, the British Library of Political and Economic Science (London School of Economics) and the Open University electronic resources library. I am especially grateful to Anne Cameron and Gary Carson of the

Local and Family History Centre History Collection at Blackpool Central Library.

A number of individuals from outside Blackpool have also contributed in different ways. Professor Janette Rutterford (Open University), and Professor James Foreman-Peck (Cardiff University) helped on issues of economic and finance history, while Professor Vanessa Toulmin (Sheffield University) opened doors to the history of the Tower. I made much use of Professor John Walton's (formerly University of Central Lancashire) work on the social history of Blackpool. Dr Sue Arthur (Leeds Metropolitan University) gave me access to her doctoral thesis on entertainment in 1930s Blackpool. Lynn Pearson's work on the development of seaside entertainments provided very useful insights. David Hill advised on issues in the Isle of Man and the Douglas Marine Drive.

Finally some friends undertook the time-consuming task of reading the first draft of the book to provide critical assessments of the contents. They provided very useful and varied insights which helped me improve the accessibility and consistency of the material. These are Jenny Batchelor, Gillian Blachford, Maximilien Génard Walton and Chris Elliott.

The quality of the book, and the accuracy of the history, derives from the generosity of these people. I remain, of course, responsible for any errors that have not been eradicated.

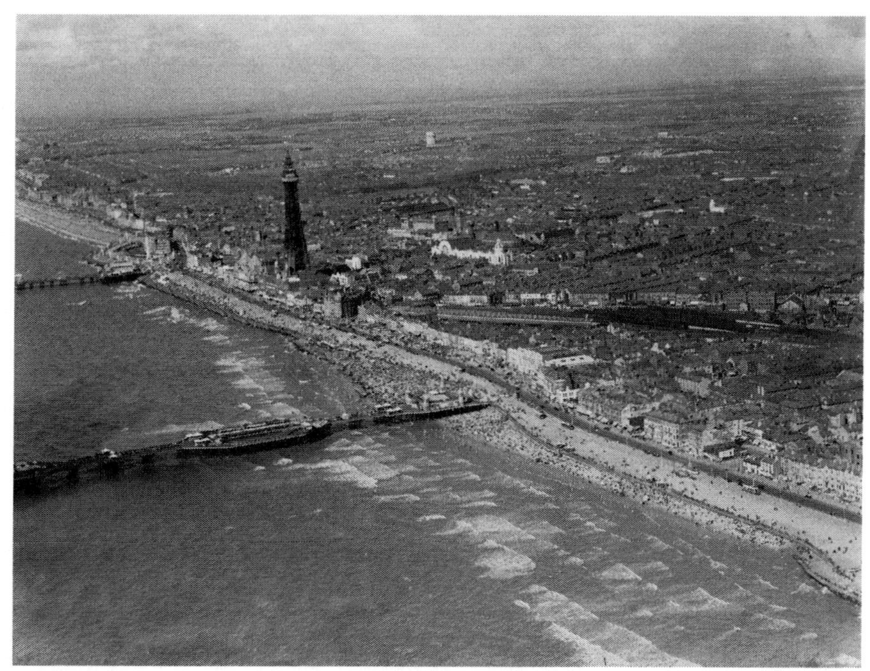

Blackpool from the air, *c.* 1934. ©Historic England licensor canmore.org.uk

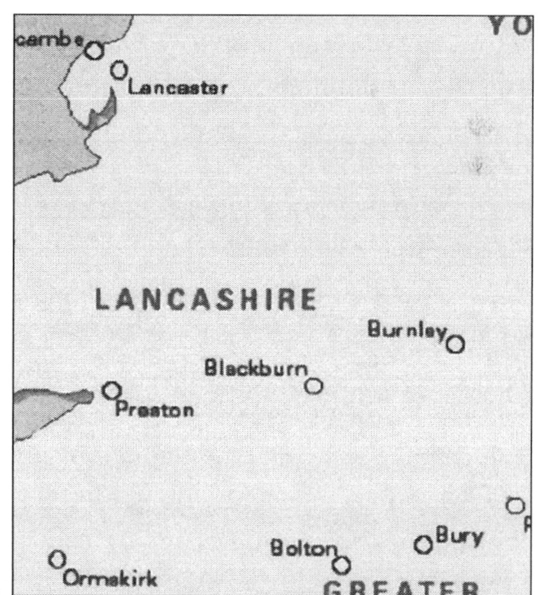

Map of Blackpool hinterland.

BLACKPOOL AND THE DEVELOPMENT OF RESORT TOWNS

This book is about the creation, success and eventual disappearance of a listed company, the Blackpool Tower Co. Ltd, which was formed in 1891 and came to be the powerhouse of the Blackpool entertainment industry when English resorts were enjoying their peak years of success. As the resort started to lose out to television and then cheap sunshine in Spain, the company was acquired by the then entertainment and electronics giant EMI in 1967 and ceased to exist as an independent entity. The underlying businesses remained in commercial ownership until they were acquired by Blackpool Council in 2010. In the heyday of the English seaside resort, Blackpool was by far the leading resort for working people's holidays. At that time the Blackpool Tower Co. dominated the entertainment business in Blackpool, just as its iconic tower dominated the physical landscape of the resort.

This is also a book about the Bickerstaffe family whose fortune was founded by Robert Bickerstaffe from small beginnings in the 1840s. John Bickerstaffe was the directing power behind the company that built the Tower and he ran it successfully with his younger brother Tom until their deaths in the 1930s when their sons took over the reins. Both brothers were also active in local politics and each rose to be mayor of Blackpool. A Bickerstaffe was chairman from the company's formation in 1891 until the resignation through ill health of Tom Bickerstaffe's son Douglas Bickerstaffe in 1961, after which the impresario Bernard Delfont played a decisive role.

While the development of all English seaside resorts did not occur to exactly the same timetable nor in the same way, the literature points to some trends which provide a framework for looking at Blackpool. Bathing in the sea was popular among some parts of society in the eighteenth century, and was also held to be good for health. Short excursions out to sea in small boats were also common. People even thought drinking seawater was good for you. Some authors suggest that over time the seaside started to attract a clientele of aristocratic and middle-class society that frequented spas such as Bath or Cheltenham.[1] This was reinforced by the interest of the British monarchy. George IV, when Prince of Wales, bought a farmhouse in Brighton in the 1780s that was replaced by the Royal Pavilion, constructed in 1815–1823. Queen Victoria bought Osborne House on the coast of the Isle of Wight in 1845.

The Arrival of the Seaside Resort 1850–1914

The railways and the industrial revolution were to make the resorts available to a much wider public, providing cheap and reasonably fast access on the one hand, and the jobs that left people enough money for an annual excursion to the seaside on the other. The rail network was sufficiently developed for Bradshaw to publish the first edition of his eponymous railway timetable in 1839. The rapid development of resort towns in England (and to an extent Wales but less so Scotland) took place from 1850 to 1914. Most of the piers that were a key feature of many resorts were built in this period, as were the ballrooms, theatres, concert halls, winter gardens, aquariums, skating rinks and latterly cinemas that grew up to provide entertainment in the evenings and in bad weather. Many bars and drinking houses sprang up as well and eventually boarding houses and hotels as the mass market moved more towards stays of several days rather than excursions on bank holidays and similar occasions.

In 1850 people amused themselves by bathing in the sea, walking or taking a carriage ride along the coast, or going for a trip in a small boat. The bathing was strictly segregated, with men and women bathing either at different times or different places on the beach, and generally was done with the use of a bathing machine.[2] The local traders (including Robert Bickerstaffe at Blackpool) made money by renting out bathing huts and plying for trade in carriages and boats, as well as supplying food and drink. Eventually seaside promenades as we know them today were built to make the seaside walks and drives more pleasant, and piers were constructed both to act as jetties for the boats and to offer a walk out across the sea.

The first pier opened in Ryde in 1814, to be followed in 1823 by a pier in Brighton and in 1830 by Southend and Walton on the Naze – all in the south of England. However the great pier building period starts with Great Yarmouth Wellington Pier in 1854, with nineteen piers opened in the 1860s, twenty in the 1870s, thirteen in the 1880s, fifteen in the 1890s and ten in the first decade of the twentieth century.[3] The piers were mostly built by local entrepreneurs and financed as public companies. At first they made money by simply charging an admission fee, but subsequently as competition arose, they hired bands to play on the pier so people would come and dance, and provided refreshment rooms. Eventually they would build concert halls, theatres and other entertainments on to the piers, and their use as jetties declined.

As visitors became more numerous, so the market for entertainment grew larger and there was more and more competition to attract the visitor's spending money. Boat trips remained popular, but became more large scale with steamboats plying between places like Llandudno and the Isle of Man. Dancing was a popular pastime and so people built ballrooms, as well as auditoriums where visiting concert parties and such entertainments would be provided. People established aquariums and similar static attractions, such as circuses, were also popular before the turn of the century. After that came more theatres and eventually cinemas.

Financing Development

This was also a period of great expansion of limited liability companies. A series of companies acts in the first half of the century had moved the legal framework from a situation where an individual act of parliament was required to start a company, towards the modern position where the promoter has to satisfy the registrar that they have complied with various formalities and agree to meet some minimum reporting requirements going forward and that is all. Very many of the seaside infrastructure projects (as also the railways before them) were financed by promoters launching a project for which they had the appropriate technical knowledge or licence or other property. They would start a public company and invite local and other subscribers to put up share capital.

An article in the *Financial Times* of 22 February 1899 wrote about such seaside entertainment schemes rather scathingly, talking about the 'peculiarities of "cheap tripper" finance'. It was however analysing a company called the 'Pyramidical Syndicate' which was proposing to build the 'Brighton Dyke Steep-Grade railway' – probably a funicular cliff railway – but had run into difficulties. One of the directors was William Darker Pitt, of whom more later. The article notes though:

> It would obviously be foolish to deny that there is money to be made out of seaside pavilions, towers, switchbacks and kindred aids to amusement. Even the Pyramidical railway might pay if run on sound lines...

As the article indicates, some of these schemes were successful but even if the seaside was booming (with the possible exception of the 1880s which was not a good decade for the UK economy), many schemes failed to raise enough money to build their attraction, and still others subsequently failed to attract enough customers to pay their way. Certainly on a more relaxed timescale than the internet boom at the turn of this century, there are, nevertheless, many parallels of people making fortunes very quickly, and others losing them just as quickly, in a context where the market did change substantially over a short period and people either guessed wrong or failed to move with the times.

The World Wars and the Depression 1914–45

The First and Second World Wars and their aftermath completely distorted the previous patterns of economic activity, not least with an increased level of taxation, and then the inter-war period was heavily affected by the Depression. This thirty-year period was therefore a challenge for seaside entrepreneurs who had to accept a turnover tax taking perhaps 15 per cent of their receipts,[4] as well as increased income taxes, and who were also challenged by significant changes in patterns of entertainment. Gramophone records and the radio changed people's domestic experience, and the cinema and Hollywood films changed their entertainment activities outside the home.

Different seaside resorts came out of the First World War differently. The lucky ones found their accommodation and public facilities taken over by the government for training and related purposes. This had the effect of bringing year-round business which boosted profits, sometimes to an embarrassing degree, since companies that profited from the war were not viewed sympathetically by the public.

The resort business depends upon being able to attract sufficient clients in a short period to justify the investment, and provide a margin to maintain the business through the rest of the year. As John Walton sums it up, it is: 'three months' hard labour and nine months' solitary confinement'.[5] The less fortunate resorts suffered, partly because the young men who were an important part of the market were in the forces, and partly because they could not find either the staff or the entertainers of the pre-war years.

Nonetheless the immediate aftermath of the First World War provided a boost to profitability with people keen to get away from the grimness of the war years. However the seaside boom was short-lived as the Depression bit in the early 1920s. In any personal budget, but particularly in that of a working-class family, daytrips to the coast and summer holidays were likely to be the first thing that was cut when earnings are short. Resorts that drew their visitors from markets that were badly hit by unemployment, such as the North East of England, had difficult trading conditions during this period.

Things started to recover but 1939 was again a bad year for resort business because a proportion of the potential visitors stayed at home as a result of the uncertainty of the political situation. Again, once war started, the resorts faced much the same situation as in the First World War, with the added problem this time that many beaches had anti-tank barriers constructed and some were even mined and shut off with barbed wire. The war again imposed distortions on the availability both of staff and entertainers. The Isle of Man, by way of example, gained by being an internment centre, but lost because the steamer services were suspended so its holiday trade all but disappeared.

This was also a period where entertainment was beginning to change. From the start of the century the music halls, where people often sat at tables and ate and drank during the performances, were replaced by conventional theatres.

In the early 20th century, new purpose-built theatres, many designed by Frank Matcham, sprang up across Britain. These were the Empires, Palaces and Hippodromes, beautiful Edwardian theatres with chandeliers, gold leaf decorations and red plush velvet seats. Unlike music halls where the audience sat at tables, the Edwardian theatres had proscenium arches, with fixed seats and separate bar and auditorium.[6]

Variety shows started to be the staple seaside fare, helped by the creation through exposure on the radio of its own stars, whom people were interested to see in the flesh. Nonetheless, these faced competition from the expanding film business:

> The popularity of variety dwindled with the advent of the talking pictures. By the 1930s many theatres had closed or become cinemas. Other forms of entertainment, such as revue, had become popular and many variety performers made their names through radio, film and later, television. In World War I many former acrobats, aerialists and jugglers were killed or injured and could no longer perform, thus robbing the stage of the breadth and variety of acts previously available.
>
> In the 1930s and 40s artists such as Ted Ray, Tommy Trinder, Nellie Wallace, Gracie Fields, Will Hay, George Formby, Sandy Powell and Max Miller appeared regularly in variety up and down the country. These were well known names made famous by radio'.[7]

Outside the resorts, the provincial theatre world was dominated by touring productions going round the Moss Empires and Stoll theatres circuits, such as the Hackney Empire or Liverpool Empire and the London Coliseum. The touring shows would also visit resort theatres during the season, where sufficiently large theatres were available. Provincial theatres were broadly split between those that hosted variety, and those where plays were performed. Variety and opera (and later musicals) tended to use larger auditoriums, which could sometimes seat as many as 2,000 people, whereas plays were generally performed in more intimate theatres. The Blackpool Opera House started out as a playhouse, and was later extensively remodelled as a variety theatre.

The Last Great Decade: the 1950s

Harold Macmillan famously said in a speech in 1957: 'Let us be frank about it, most of our people have never had it so good.' This growth in the standard of living, was, however, to be very problematical for the resorts. First there was television and then eventually they faced strong competition from foreign tourism, with Spain in particular offering cheap sea, sand and drink with sunshine seemingly guaranteed and a much higher class of accommodation than the English boarding houses. In a sense, as Beeching's report on the railways in 1963 also reflected, the country's infrastructure was showing the disadvantages of having been a prime mover, with its assets now old and outdated, and with little investment in reshaping for the future, thanks in part to the World Wars.

After the Second World War there was again a mini-boom as people returning from the war wanted to enjoy again some of their pre-war pleasures. Not all seaside towns were able to enjoy success immediately because their resorts had in effect been shut down during the war and much work was needed to bring them back into working condition. Nevertheless the 1950s were a decade where the English resorts prospered. The steamer trip had declined, as had the ballrooms, albeit with some notable exceptions, but variety, plays and cinema were all in demand. Some resorts such as Whitley Bay and Blackpool also had major permanent fairground attractions as a significant part of their armoury. Circuses, zoos and aquariums were also to an extent starting to decline.

However, people's patterns of entertainment were most hit by the arrival of television in the 1950s, and particularly with the expansion of broadcasting when commercial television companies were granted licenses in 1957. Television did not spread quickly at first, as sets were expensive and the broadcasting limited, but it did grow steadily, and started to give people the alternative of being entertained in their own homes instead of going out.

The theatre world generally, and the touring theatres in particular, could not sustain the competition from a combination of television and cinema. The Stoll and Moss theatre circuits shed their less sustainable venues in this period and the big 'No 1 Tour' productions melted away. In the resorts more emphasis was put on variety shows produced uniquely for the resort, which featured radio and then television stars as the headliners, and played just for the main part of the summer season. The 'summer stock' repertory company disappeared.

Over time many theatres were taken into public ownership as towns and cities acted to try to preserve at least some of the entertainment which was part of attracting good visitor numbers. By the 1970s the audience was slipping away to warmer climes and only Blackpool, Great Yarmouth, Bournemouth and Torquay could sustain summer variety with the top comedians and singers of the day playing twice nightly; and other resorts maintained shows, but usually less expensively-produced and with less well-known artists as top of the bill.

The impact of growing competition was not immediately felt by all the resorts – in the 1960s the foreign package holiday impacted only the middle classes. These were a relatively small proportion of the total visitor market, but would of course fall most heavily on those resorts where they formed a particular focus. These had already suffered up to a point as Devon and Cornwall developed their seaside business. Resorts such as Blackpool and Great Yarmouth that catered for a large working class market did not immediately feel the competition.

Eventually the resorts had to reinvent themselves, with accommodation raised to a higher standard, and the focus more on short stay visitors who were probably on average older than their 1950s counterparts. Even in the largest resorts the supply of entertainment was reduced and often disco replaced a live performance.

The Development of Blackpool

John Walton[8] describes Blackpool as 'Britain's largest, brashest, busiest and best-publicised resort'. He says 'It became ... the Mecca of the English working class on pleasure bent during the half-century or so after 1870, starting as a magnet for cotton workers and extending its spell nationwide ... by the inter-war years.' If Manchester is the cradle of the industrial revolution, then Blackpool was its playground, as the industrial workers of the North West chose the town as their principal seaside resort.

While Blackpool was far from being among the first resorts developed in the UK, it became an archetype: it was popular enough to see the development, and often on a more magnificent scale, of all and any entertainments that could be found in other resorts. For example, Blackpool has three piers, whereas other towns were generally content with one or at most two. The very scope of its offerings, quite apart from its beaches and sea, enhanced its lure for the visitor. The Blackpool Tower, indeed, is iconic for the town, and an example of its ability to mount bigger and better diversions than other resorts. Entrepreneurs were willing to try out all sorts of new ideas in Blackpool's heyday. In keeping with the spirit of the times, some went broke very quickly, but some made a fortune for their promoters.

Blackpool was a very minor resort in the eighteenth century. It had miles of sandy beaches, facing the Irish Sea. Walton[9] describes it in the late eighteenth century as 'a line of scattered houses, well-filled with a few hundred August visitors, drawn from the mercantile and professional classes of Lancashire and the West Riding of Yorkshire, with a leavening of gentry, farmers and textile manufacturers.' He says that even by 1841 Blackpool had little more than 1,000 regular inhabitants and was full in mid-August with just over 3,000 visitors. He contrasts this with Brighton's resident population of 40,000 at the time. The town continued to grow, however, drawing its public from the expanding Lancashire middle classes, augmented at weekends in high summer by trippers from the cotton towns.

Blackpool sits on a straight beach that runs for about 18 miles north/south, from Fleetwood in the north down to Lytham. The beach shelves relatively gently, so it is comfortable and safe for bathing; the sea withdraws a distance at low tide, but comes right back to the promenade at high water, providing additional sport for some in avoiding the incoming water. However, the long beach sits at the western edge of land, known as the Fylde, jutting into the Irish Sea and bounded to the north by the River Wyre and to the south by the Ribble. Its geographical location means that the main road system, and initially the rail system, bypass it to the east, with the county town of Preston, 20 miles from Blackpool, on the main transport arteries. Anyone wishing to make a daytrip to Blackpool before the arrival of the railway was therefore faced with a lengthy road journey.

The town was, however, the accidental beneficiary of a visionary scheme conceived by Sir Peter Hesketh-Fleetwood. His idea was to create a new town – Fleetwood – on the estuary of the Wyre, where he had a large amount of land. The development was to be a railhead for the London Euston line, with passengers taking steamers from there to Scotland, Ireland and the Isle of Man (said to be visible from Blackpool on a clear day). It was also intended to be a luxurious resort. Hesketh-Fleetwood hired Decimus Burton to build a luxury hotel (The North Euston Hotel, still in existence) and design the town. He also built the Preston and Wyre Railway, which connected Fleetwood to Preston and linked it to the rail systems giving access to the industrial hinterland in Lancashire and West Yorkshire.

The railway opened in 1840 and formed part of the main London to Glasgow route according to Turner and Palmer.[10] They say, however, that after two years the business was failing and the railway company hit on the idea of running cheap excursions to the coast. These were successful, but many people wanted to go to Blackpool, not Fleetwood. The line ran almost parallel to the coast, but two or three miles inland. Trippers heading for Blackpool had to leave the train at Poulton-le-Fylde (north-east of Blackpool), and walk or find other transport for the four miles remaining.[11] According to Turner and Palmer, this could lead to disappointments and disagreements, and people were quickly convinced that a branch line should be built from Poulton to Blackpool. In 1846 the first station in Blackpool was opened at Talbot Road (Turner and Palmer[12]) and in effect the stage was set for the development of Blackpool as a popular resort.

Although Blackpool had been a small centre for sea-bathing and boat trips for some decades, administratively it did not exist, and was geographically in the district of Layton with Warbreck. It had no water supplies beyond a few wells, no sanitation, no gas or electricity and no planning constraints. As the tripper trade mushroomed with the advent of the railway, and bars and catering businesses were set up to profit from it, it became clear that collective action needed to be taken to address environmental concerns and avoid driving away the tourists through the bad physical conditions. This indeed has been a recurring feature of the town: those who profited from the tourist trade were progressively willing to work together to improve the infrastructure for the general good.

The first initiative in this direction was the creation of a Local Board of Health in 1851. This had nine locally-elected members and its aim was to improve the infrastructure. Its early activities included making the first attempt to consolidate the promenade, as both a tourist facility and a sea defence. It also installed some gas street lighting, having started a gasworks in 1854. Attempts were made to form a company to provide fresh water, and although this had difficulty in attracting investment, the Fylde Waterworks started successfully in 1864.

There was significant growth in the entertainment infrastructure as well. From 1861 the first 'amusement centre' was created on the cliffs above the north shore, offering food and drink as well as dancing and recitals. This was called Uncle Tom's Cabin, and provided an example to be followed by other businesses more central to Blackpool in the 1870s. This was followed in 1863 by an even more significant creation: the North Pier was the first of the town's eventual three piers to be built. Not only was it the first major physical tourist attraction, but it was also financed by the creation of a public company, with money raised from Blackpool and the surrounding region. Walton[13] says: 'Nearly 30 per cent of the shares were taken by Blackpool people, a further 22 per cent from nearby Preston, and almost all the rest were purchased by investors from Blackpool's established Lancashire catchment area, with a considerable Manchester presence.'

Company law had gone through a number of rapid changes from 1844 to 1862 to facilitate the raising of risk capital by public subscription through the creation of small listed companies. These were generally listed on a regional exchange – the centralisation on the London Stock Exchange only took place a century later. Many people were willing to invest in local companies whose operations they could see and whose business model they understood. They invested primarily because they were looking for a continuing dividend stream, they were not intent on speculation in the share price.

The model for the Blackpool companies was that they had a year-end of 30 September or 31 October, at the end of the summer season. They rapidly drew up the annual statements (often in less than a month, which is still today a challenge for even the most sophisticated multinationals), held the annual shareholders' meeting, and paid the dividend. John Bickerstaffe, chairman of the Blackpool Tower Co., even joked to shareholders when proposing to move the year-end back from October to September, which would have meant they would get their dividend a month earlier. There was little or no business activity in the winter months, and no interim dividend.

Most of Blackpool's leisure infrastructure developments were funded in this way. Each of the three piers were built by listed companies: the Blackpool Pier Co. (North Pier), the Blackpool South Jetty Co. (Central Pier) and the Victoria Pier Co. (South Pier). The Winter Gardens was similarly a listed company, and the Alhambra, as well, of course, as the Blackpool Tower Co. There were also tram companies and hotel companies.

Turner and Palmer[14] speak of 'the great Blackpool boom of the 1870s'. The resort developed rapidly. The South Jetty Co. opened its pier in 1868 starting out from land on the central beach given them by Robert Bickerstaffe, in front of his Wellington Hotel. The piers have changed names over the years, and the South Jetty (one of whose principal functions was to act as a departure point for steamer trips) eventually became the Central Pier when the third pier opened on South beach. This was followed by work to consolidate the promenade (a continuing source of debate for the local authority and ratepayers) in 1870. The Raikes Hall Park Gardens and Aquarium Co. was founded in 1871 and opened Raikes Hall pleasure gardens in 1872. This became the main source of entertainment for visitors at that time, it offered dancing, food and drink, and firework displays accompanying topical tableaux or parades.

In 1872 Dr W. H. Cocker (the scion of a prominent Blackpool family that dominated much of the development of the town in the nineteenth century) built an aquarium on the sea front between the two piers. In 1875 the Blackpool Winter Gardens Co. was launched to build an amusement centre a short distance back from the beach near what is now the main railway station. This opened in 1878 and was to remain a significant entertainment centre and eventually house one of the most important theatres. Its success also signalled future problems for Raikes Hall, which was neither central nor on the sea front. The North Pier Co. responded to competition by building an 'Indian Pavilion' at the sea end, which was used for recitals.

There were one or two theatres in Blackpool as well, but these were not well supported. Only when Thomas Sergenson took a five-year lease of the Prince of Wales Theatre in 1880 and then also took on the Theatre Royal was there profitable theatrical entertainment. This may have motivated the Winter Gardens Co. to build its own theatre – the Opera House, which opened in 1889 with performances of The Yeomen of the Guard by the D'Oyly Carte Co. This also signalled the arrival on the Blackpool scene of William Holland, as the new general manager of the Winter Gardens Co., who was to be a key figure in Blackpool entertainment. Sergenson went on to build the Grand Theatre, close to the Winter Gardens, which opened in 1894 and had been designed by Frank Matcham.

In 1876 Blackpool achieved the status of a borough. Dr Cocker was chairman of the local Conservative association, which won most of the seats in the first municipal elections, and became the first mayor of Blackpool. The town was able to move forward in a more organised manner as the new council enforced building regulations, ran a police force, consolidated the promenade, oversaw sanitation and water and eventually brought in electric light and the electric tramway.

The council also took a very active role in advertising the resort and trying to encourage visitors. It worked to encourage the development of the railways. What would today be seen as evident conflicts of interest between public and private roles seem to have been commonplace at the time, with major local business figures, such as Dr Cocker, also playing prominent roles in the affairs of the town council. At the time this does not seem to have been thought problematical, with the entrepreneurs' private interests mirroring the interests of most of the citizens, and running parallel to the interests of the town as a whole.

Blackpool can be seen as an artificial creation, with only a very small indigenous population at the beginning of the nineteenth century, drawing to it people whose main interest was to earn money through different aspects of the tourist trade. There were very few banks or lawyers and related professional activities and it had no hospital. Consequently it may well be that it would have been difficult to find anyone eligible to stand for the council who was not in the tourist business. The time demands would also limit candidates to those who could afford to take time away from their main business activity.

2

THE BICKERSTAFFE FAMILY

John Bickerstaffe (later Sir John): justice of the peace, freemason, councillor, alderman, and mayor of Blackpool, even some time president of Blackpool Football Club, was the driving force behind the development of the Blackpool Tower, and chaired the Blackpool Tower Co. from 1891 until his death in 1930. He was born in Blackpool, educated there, and became a dominant force in the business community of the resort, with interests in several ventures. Born into a family of relatively modest means, he became a member of the emergent wealthy middle class: he was in many ways a typical Victorian entrepreneur, apparently with a golden touch.

He was born in 1848, when the railway had already reached Blackpool and when his father (Robert) was laying the foundation of the family fortune, based on the growth of the town as a resort. John Bickerstaffe was a second generation entrepreneur who worked with his father, but developed the family business far beyond what his father had started. There were many Bickerstaffes active in Blackpool, but the main protagonists in the commerce of the resort were Robert Bickerstaffe Snr, his sons John and Tom, and his nephew Robert Bickerstaffe (hereafter 'Cousin Bob') who worked together in different combinations in a number of enterprises. John, Tom and Cousin Bob were all Blackpool councillors at one time or another, and Tom eventually became a director of the Blackpool Tower Co. and succeeded John as chairman. Tom Bickerstaffe was also involved in the development of the Belle Vue entertainment park in Manchester.

Curiously, the Bickerstaffes and other local families who were the key developers of the resort in the nineteenth century, seem not to be particularly recognised in modern day Blackpool, and there is, for example, no book on the Bickerstaffes, even though there are many about the resort in general and its piers and theatres as well as the Tower, in particular. There are, however, acres of contemporary press coverage in what, a hundred years ago, was a thriving collection of local newspapers. Fortunately a local journalist, Ben Bowman, had the idea to write a series of articles about the Bickerstaffes in the *Blackpool Gazette* and *Herald* in 1924. These preserved some of the detail of the family's early life.

Bowman says that a John Bickerstaffe (grandfather of John, Tom and Cousin Bob) was born in 1760 and lived in Blackpool until 1845 – a formidable lifespan for the period. His wife lived to the age of eighty-four, so the clan had genes that offered longevity. The *Blackpool Gazette* (15 November 1889) says that 'The Bickerstaffes appear to have been indigenous to the soil of Blackpool and to have been bred and born "between wind and water"'. The paper says 'in the farthest off times of which there is any record, there were Bickerstaffes who earned a precarious livelihood by fishing in the rough waters of the western coast.' It adds that (Grandfather) John Bickerstaffe was a seafaring man.

Of Grandfather John's children, Edward, the eldest was the father of Cousin Bob (born 1831), and the second son was Robert Snr, born 1807. Bowman says the two sons when adults lived nearby each other in cottages on the sea front. Edward worked in transport and contracting but Robert Snr was a waterman, and his first step into the resort business was taking visitors out to sea on pleasure trips in a small rowing boat (*Blackpool Herald* 15 Aug 1879). From this he was able to buy, with a brother, a

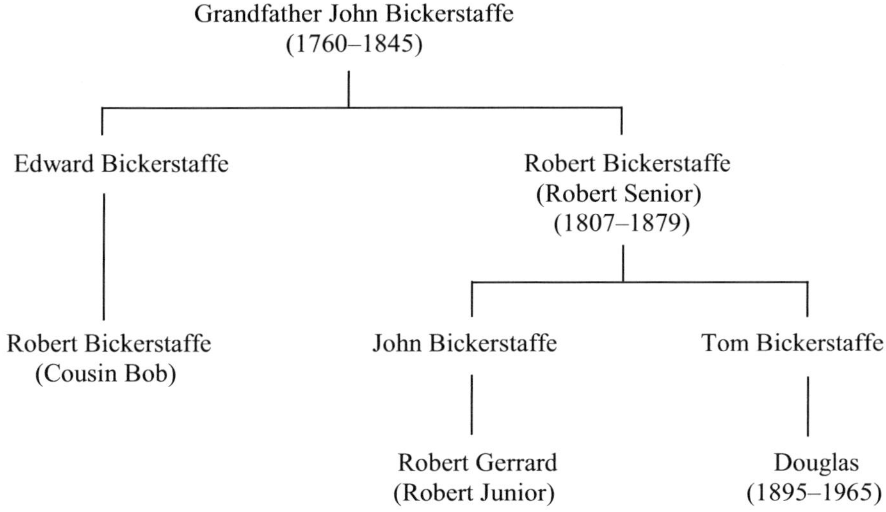

Bickerstaffe family tree.

bathing machine – he is quoted as saying it was only the third in the place. Moving on from there, he bought a sail-boat.

The Wellington Hotel

Robert Senior's first major step as an entrepreneur was to build the Wellington Hotel, on the sea front in an area known as Lower Blackpool at the time. He bought a 'pinfold' (cattle enclosure) on the south beach with the idea of developing it as a landing and storage area for his boating and sea trip business. He is quoted as having asked the landowner's agent how much he wanted. The agent, Thomas Fair, asked how much money he had, to which he replied '£40'. They settled for £40 on the spot, to be followed by a further £40 in a year's time. However, Bickerstaffe quickly saw the potential to establish the hotel (probably more like a public house initially) on that piece of land to provide facilities for boatmen and their customers.

His obituary (1879) quotes a speech he made twenty-five years later in 1875: 'I was so encouraged in my business that I commenced to build the Wellington Hotel, but I found I was £500 short to build and furnish it; consequently I had to borrow.' It can be seen that he was either a massive risk-taker or very confident that he could make the money: his debt to equity ratio would have been 540-40 at the start of the project, at 13.5 to 1 an astonishing amount of leverage. The debt could be equivalent to about £1 million at today's prices. It is unlikely he got the money from a bank as banking was sketchy at best at the time; it is more likely that he was financed partly by a brewery and borrowed from another entrepreneur, who must have had great confidence in Robert's ability. Blackpool was seriously underdeveloped at that time, and the year, 1850, marked the beginning of the construction of what we could recognise as modern Blackpool, so the moment was well chosen.

As he later said: 'I paid it off as soon as I could. I built several houses near the Wellington Hotel, and buildings commenced to spring up all over the place.' The Wellington Hotel was to play a key role in the development of his business. As noted, he had to borrow a lot of money to do this, but he successfully paid it off and made money to build more properties in the vicinity. One of these became an ironmongers run by one of his brothers.

Edward's son, Cousin Bob, also lived with Robert Snr, and worked in the hotel and in the pleasure boat business. Bowman says that Cousin Bob had been sent to Blackburn in about 1844 to work in a draper's shop, but had not liked the trade and returned to Blackpool to work with his uncle as a boatman. Cousin Bob's mother had died and his father had remarried, so it may be the arrangement was more comfortable for all concerned. In any event, Cousin Bob worked alongside his uncle, Robert Snr, in developing the Wellington Hotel site and the pleasure boats, and eventually alongside his younger cousin, John, born in 1848.

The next big venture for Robert Snr was promoting the Central Pier, as it is now known. He continued to operate his pleasure boat business, but this too evolved with the resort. In 1863 the

Blackpool Pier Co. opened what is now the North Pier. The business model was that the more well-to-do visitors could pay an entrance fee and then walk along the pier, taking the sea air in comfort. The beach at Blackpool shelves very slowly, so it is difficult to launch small boats at low water, and larger ships could not come close. Consequently the construction of the pier offered the opportunity for larger boats to dock at the sea extremity, where extension jetties were built, and before long steamer trips to the Isle of Man, Llandudno, Southport and other resorts were being offered from the North Pier.

The South Jetty Co.

The land used by the Wellington Hotel had been shored up to make an easier launch site, but Robert Snr's ambitions moved on to the idea of building a jetty out into the sea to offer steamer trips and to meet the competition from the North Pier operators. Robert worked with other entrepreneurs to promote what became the South Jetty Co., a local, listed company, after the fashion of the times. He gave the company land in front of the Wellington Hotel from which to build out to sea.

Turner and Palmer[1] say that the South Jetty Co. owed its origins to directors of the Blackpool Pier Co., who wanted to build on the success of the North Pier. Although this idea was championed by Major Francis Preston, a Manchester engineer who chaired the Pier Co., they could not persuade their fellow directors, so the South Jetty Co. was formed, including six of the former directors of the Blackpool Pier Co.

The South Jetty opened in 1868. Turner and Palmer say 'It was not long before the pessimism of the North Pier directors was proved to be justified. The new pier was too far from the centre of the town in those days to attract anything like the numbers who patronised the North Pier.' They say that Cousin Bob told the story later of his uncle carrying £1,000 in sovereigns across from the Wellington Hotel to get the company over a cash crisis.

Robert Snr's later comments (made in 1875 at a banquet to celebrate extensions to the Wellington Hotel) were: 'There was very little confidence in the company at that time, and £10 shares were sold for £5. We could not get a steamer to come near, so I agitated for two new steamers. I promised to get one myself if the company would get one also. They promised to do so. I ordered the steamer *Wellington* to be built at Mr. Alsupp's, Preston.'

In the end it was Cousin Bob who rescued the South Jetty. He had left his uncle's business in 1853 when he got married, and operated independently as a waterman (and as the first coxswain of the Blackpool lifeboat from 1864, so the press sometimes referred to him as 'Coxn. Bob'). In 1869 he opened a refreshment room on the South Jetty and in 1870 was appointed manager of the pier.

Cousin Bob decided on a bold gesture: he offered visitors free access to the pier and a daytrip to Southport of one shilling (against the North Pier price of two shillings). He also hit on the idea of engaging a brass band that happened to be in the resort to play at the end of the pier. Turner and Palmer report that when the boat came back, the band was playing, and the passengers stayed on the pier all evening to dance. They say that this marked the turning point in the South Jetty's fortunes, and also marked the offer of an entertainment aimed specifically at the working class – 'dancing was the great preoccupation of the Lancashire working classes'. Cousin Bob even styled the Jetty 'The People's Pier'.

Robert Snr reported in his 1875 speech that the South Jetty Co. had not kept their promise to buy a steamer, and he had had to hire two steamers to supplement the *Wellington*. However, as the Jetty Co. started to make money, the company bought the *Wellington* from him and also commissioned a new steamer.

From being heavily indebted in 1850, by 1868 Robert Snr as in a position to help promote the South Jetty Co., to loan it money and to finance the purchase of a steamer to develop the jetty business. In fact once the jetty was operating effectively, it increased business at the Wellington such that he had to increase the size of the premises – which is what he was celebrating in 1875. The 1840 waterman was a successful local entrepreneur by 1870. This is a testament to the rapid growth of Blackpool at that time, and Robert's willingness to take risks to profit from that.

It should not be forgotten that his son John was born in 1848. He would have had no recollection of the founding of the Wellington Hotel, but grew up living there. When the South Jetty opened in 1868 he would have been twenty years old, and undoubtedly involved in his father's business. He would have seen at first hand the creation of the South Jetty Co. – probably lasting three or four years – the difficulty of getting it going, the falling share price, the cash flow crises, the need to acquire assets not in the budget and then its eventual success once the right formula was found. This experience was to stand him in good stead from 1891 to 1894 as chairman of the Blackpool Tower Co.

Robert Bickertsaffe Senior's last investment was in another steamer, called the *Bickerstaffe* (the family, while very creative in business, seemingly were not so when it came to names). This was built at Laird Brothers Birkenhead (later Cammel Laird) and its 1879 maiden voyage was reported in the *East Lancashire Gazette* (and also the *Liverpool Mercury* of 26 May 1879). The paper described it as 'a very handsome iron paddle steamer' whose dimensions were 100 feet in length, 22 feet 6 inches in beam, with a depth, deck to keel, of 8 feet 6 inches and drawing 5 feet. They said it was designed for excursions from Blackpool ('one of the prettiest watering places in the North of England') to Douglas, Llandudno, Barrow in Furness, Southport and other places of interest. The paper says the boat was commissioned by Robert and John Bickerstaffe. The maiden cruise was from Birkenhead to Blackpool South Jetty and carried a large party including much of Blackpool Council (among them Councillor Robert Bickerstaffe – Cousin Bob). When it arrived in Blackpool, there were thousands of people waiting to see it.

The paper reports that lunch was served during the 90-minute voyage and included numerous toasts, as was the custom at the time. William Laird wished the new owners well. John Bickerstaffe responded, saying he and his father were very satisfied by the boat and noting that 'although the tender received from Laird Brothers was higher than any other received, the owners of the *Bickerstaffe* preferred paying more money in order to ensure a thoroughly good boat that would give satisfaction in every respect'. This principle of buying only the best was a hallmark of John Bickerstaffe's management: he would go on later to hire Frank Matcham, the outstanding theatre architect of the era, to design the Tower Circus and the Tower ballroom. There is no way of knowing if it was his father's view, passed on, or his own contribution, but in the future, when he took on new projects, he spent lavishly to get high quality and was generally rewarded by commercial success.

Robert Bickerstaffe Snr died on 7 August 1879, aged seventy-two. His obituary quotes him as saying once: 'When I was a boy I could have told every man and woman's name in the place, and most of their children's.' He added that at that time there was no church or school or shop. By the time of his death, Blackpool was a thriving seaside resort, serving in particular the Lancashire industrial towns but also drawing visitors from West Yorkshire and as far South as Birmingham and had achieved the status of a borough. He had lived through this massive growth and profited from it, owning the Wellington Hotel and the *Bickerstaffe* steamer as well as having played a significant role in the South Jetty. He had given his son John a remarkable first-hand business education and provided him with a good financial base.

John Bickerstaffe

The *Blackburn Standard* of 4 January 1890 published a pen portrait of John Bickerstaffe to mark the start of his first term as mayor of Blackpool. The paper says he was educated first at the

Blackpool National Schools and then at a private establishment also in Blackpool. He went to work as a boatman, and with his cousin, formed part of the lifeboat crew from time to time. The journalist writes: 'Like his father, he began at the foot of the ladder of life, and by his persevering habits, his shrewd common sense and business tact, he has ascended rung by rung, until he now occupies the most dignified and honourable position at the disposal of his fellow townsmen.'

Saying he started at the foot of the ladder may, of course, be Victorian hyperbole, given his father owned the Wellington Hotel. The paper relates that the extension of the Wellington Hotel was the opportunity for John Bickerstaffe to take a share in that business. In 1874 he married into a Lancashire family (and went on to father seven daughters and one son). He took over management of the Wellington before his father's death, and was a founder member of the Blackpool & Fylde Licensed Victuallers' Association (hotel-keepers' trade association) when it started in 1878.

This was a period of a great expansion in his interests. When Blackpool had become a borough, Cousin Bob had been elected a councillor in the first elections. However, Cousin Bob did not choose to stand for re-election at the end of his term, citing too much pressure on his time while he was also running the South Jetty and steamers. This first step by a family member into local politics must have encouraged John to stand and in 1880 he was elected councillor for the Brunswick ward of the borough, where he lived.

He stood as a Conservative candidate and polled 214 votes (*Blackpool Gazette and News*, 5 November 1880) against his opponent's 125, gaining, according to the paper, the largest majority of any candidate. The paper reports that the defeated candidate (Jabez Kay) had recently prosecuted a boy for taking a turnip from his fields. Bickerstaffe's campaign included having a procession of boys carry turnips through the ward: 'the whole performance caused considerable amusement in the locality'.

Bickerstaffe entered into the life of the council with vigour. It would be commonplace today for a local council, especially in a seaside resort, to have a budget to promote the town to the outside world. It was, however, unusual in the nineteenth century and Blackpool was remarkable for having decided, even before being incorporated as a borough, that promoting the resort was an appropriate and indeed necessary civic activity.

It is an example of the way at the time that local businessmen promoted their own interests but also the public good. People did not appear to find any conflict of interest, and were comfortable that businessmen could also be local politicians and philanthropists, as was the case with John Bickerstaffe. As a councillor, Bickerstaffe served as chairman of the advertising committee, whose function was to promote the resort. He also served on the markets, gas and sanitary committees.

Bickerstaffe's commercial interests flourished from the time when he began to take over from his father. He had a direct stake in the *Bickerstaffe* as we have seen. He became a director of the South Jetty Co. The *Blackburn Standard* said in its mayoral portrait that: 'Nearly the whole of Mr Bickerstaffe's great wealth is invested in his native town, he being proprietor of the Wellington and Victoria hotels, a director of the Electric Tramway Co., a large shareholder in the Winter Gardens, the Royal Palace Gardens[2] and other local companies.'

In addition he had supported local associations, becoming a founder and president of the Blackpool Football Club (which famously was later the team of Stanley Matthews). He also erected the Victoria Schools (in the area of town behind the South Jetty), at a reported cost to himself of £1,200, to provide accommodation for day and Sunday schools, and was a pillar of the Church of England. He was also a freemason, being a member of two local lodges. The *Isle of Man Times* (8 September 1883) reports that Bickerstaffe and Cousin Bob asked the Blackpool council to give the street sweepers and night soil men a day off so that the Bickerstaffes could give them a daytrip to Douglas in their steamer.

John was a keen traveller. The *Blackburn Standard* says that 'he has travelled a great deal, having visited most of the Continental countries. In 1882–3, in company with his brother, Mr T. Bickerstaffe, he made a tour of Egypt and Palestine, spending Christmas Eve in the church built over the spot where Christ was born.' He continued throughout his life to make the most of the seasonal nature of Blackpool business.

John Bickerstaffe was made an alderman[3] in 1887 and accepted nomination as the mayor of Blackpool in 1889. When his election was announced the *Blackpool Gazette* wrote: 'Undoubtedly Mr Alderman John Bickerstaffe possesses every one of those qualifications which go to make up a successful Mayor.' The *Blackburn Standard* wrote: 'Though not exactly handsome, Mr Bickerstaffe has a fine, open countenance, and his spacious brow and clear-cut features indicate pretty faithfully his intellectuality, frankness and geniality of disposition. The secret of his great popularity lies in his unobtrusiveness, his open, generous nature, his willingness to mix and associate with all sections of the community. The hardy boatman and humble labourer stand as high in the estimation of Mr Bickerstaffe, from a social standpoint, as do those blessed with an amplitude of fortune, or basking in the sunshine of official distinction.'

It was apparently the custom for the term of office of a new mayor to start with a civic banquet. The *Gazette* reported that Bickerstaffe respected the tradition and provided a banquet at the Wellington Hotel. The paper describes this as 'the most sumptuous feast that has yet taken place in Blackpool'. It was also the occasion of his forty-second birthday and his fourteenth wedding anniversary.

In July that year John Bickerstaffe offered his civic colleagues another treat: a daytrip in the *Bickerstaffe* to Beaumaris and the Menai suspension bridge. The party left the South Jetty at 9 a.m., landed at 2 p.m. near the bridge, leaving at 5 p.m. and docking at 10 p.m. The *Gazette* says 'Refreshments were lavishly provided on board by the Mayor, and the variety of the wines and the eatables gave every satisfaction'. The guests included his council colleagues, but also officials from the Lancashire Football Association, representatives of towns such as Southport, Bolton and Preston as well as directors of the Electric Tramway Co. and the South Jetty Co. and, of course, Cousin Bob. John Bickerstaffe did not know it, but he was to embark upon the most perilous voyage in his life before the year was out.

The Younger Bickerstaffes

Tom Bickerstaffe was twelve years younger than John. Like his brother he was elected as a councillor, later becoming both an alderman and eventually mayor. He worked hard on the council and is credited with the idea of the Blackpool illuminations. He joined the Tower Co. board in 1911. He had a reasonably substantial shareholding in the Winter Gardens Co. and played a key role in the takeover of the Winter Gardens by the Tower Co. in 1928. He took over the chair of the Tower Co. when John died in 1930, but passed away himself, after a heart attack at a railway station in Manchester, in 1934.

Robert Bickerstaffe Jnr (Robert Gerrard Bickerstaffe) was John's only son, born in 1875. He moved to Liverpool where he practised as a solicitor. He took his father's seat on the Tower Co. board in 1930 and succeeded Tom as chairman in 1934. He ran the company throughout the Second World War, but resigned for health reasons in 1947 and died in 1948.

The final Bickerstaffe chairman was Douglas, Tom's son, born in 1895. He lived most of his life in Blackpool and had various entertainment interests. He ran his father's steamers until the industry declined sharply in the 1930s. Douglas joined the Tower Co. board in 1937, and became chairman in 1947. He resigned as chair in 1961 but remained on the board until 1964, and died in 1965.

3

A TALE OF TWO TOWERS

The Isle of Man, William Darker Pitt and the Standard Contract and Debenture Corporation
The idea for the construction of the Blackpool Tower came from the Isle of Man, in the form of a scheme promoted by the Standard Contract and Debenture Corporation, and its managing director, William Darker Pitt. The literature is not kind to Darker Pitt, treating him as a fraudster and serial promoter of seaside entertainments where investors lost their money. A series of three articles in the *Financial Times* of 16, 18 and 23 February 1899 lampooned the 'Pyramidical Syndicate', run by Darker Pitt, and the numerous attractions (Pyramidical Railway, Caudrey's Steeplechase, the Conical Gliding Tower, etc.) for which it had licences and the resorts (Margate, Southend, Blackpool), where it said it had sites to operate them.

It is not, however, clear that Darker Pitt originally set out to defraud through chains of interlinked companies which entered into profitable contracts with each other, creating a mirage of apparently successful ventures with no real substance. He may well have started out simply as a seller of business ideas, and progressively run into financing problems. His ideas were quite creative, and, given solid financial backing and good management, could easily have resulted in prosperous businesses, as in the case of the Blackpool Tower Co.

Even the *Financial Times* comments (23 February 1899, p5): 'It would be foolish to deny that there is money to be made out of seaside pavilions, towers, switchbacks and kindred aids to amusement. Even the Pyramidical railway might make money if run on sound lines, and Caudrey's Switchback Steeplechase might yield a small fortune if constructed with due regard to correct gradients. But there has been something radically wrong with the Pyramidical Syndicate throughout its career and it seems to have imparted the defect to practically everything it has touched. The history of the Blackpool Tower is useful as illustrating the possibility of rescuing an undertaking of the kind from the effects of undesirable auspices.'

William (in some documents Walter) Darker Pitt was probably quite unlucky, but he also probably pushed his schemes too hard and too far. If he had been working in the early twenty-first century, he might well have had a successful career in an investment bank, coming up with creative schemes into which the bank invited its private investors to put money. Unfortunately, he was an independent operator, without deep financial pockets, and generally relied upon the flotation of small companies to buy schemes from him and take them forward. He often had too many schemes in hand at the same time. These schemes were profitable or not as a function (a) of their success or otherwise in raising money, and (b) the presence or not of a shareholder who was willing to take the project on and make it work. Unfortunately for Darker Pitt, most of the time these conditions were not present.

The central idea behind the creation of the Standard Contract and Debenture Corporation, Darker Pitt's operating entity for the period that concerns us, was the Eiffel Tower, or at least the idea, demonstrated by the French original, that a tower could be a significant tourist attraction. The Eiffel Tower had opened in 1889 to great commercial success. It had been designed by Eiffel engineers and had won a competition to be the centre piece of the 1889 World's Fair in Paris. During the construction period it had attracted a lot of press coverage and was swamped with visitors willing to pay an admission fee when it opened. It still receives 7 million visitors a year. The Eiffel Tower was rumoured to be vastly profitable and to have recovered its construction cost in its first year (actually within two years, as its promoters later told John Bickerstaffe).

Darker Pitt evidently saw this as a great idea to adapt within the general area of promoting seaside resort amusements. However, the idea was not to replicate the Eiffel Tower physically, but rather to exploit the idea that people would pay to go up a tower. Coincidentally, lift technology had recently advanced to the point where this could be done without climbing stairs. Darker Pitt went on to propose towers in both Blackpool and Douglas, Isle of Man.

The Eiffel Tower is just over 1,000 feet high, and is an elegant stand-alone structure. The Blackpool Tower is, however, only 500 feet high, with its legs encased in buildings – the architects wanted to provide an anchoring weight, given the sandy nature of the terrain. For that matter the proposed Douglas Tower was linked to a suspension bridge across Douglas harbour. From a business point of view, one might observe people would probably pay just as much money for ascending a 500-foot tower as a 1,000-foot one, so there was no point in incurring the extra construction cost. Maxwell and Tuke, the architects of the Blackpool Tower, commented elsewhere that a tower of 1,000 feet would require four times the ironwork of a 500-foot tower.

Standard Contract and Debenture Corporation

F. K. Pearson[1] says that Darker Pitt had already been active in the Isle of Man. He reports that, together with a solicitor, Darker Pitt had bought the Douglas Bay Tramway in 1882, promoted the formation of a new company, Isle of Man Tramways Ltd., and sold the line to the new company. In 1889 Darker Pitt turned up again in the Isle of Man, accompanied by Dr William Abbotts and Frederick Darlington (apparently a London-based engineer). They registered at least three companies:

Standard Contract and Debenture Corporation (authorised share capital of £100,000, later raised to £500,000 but according to the liquidator only £730 actually paid up), which was their main operating company;

Douglas Head Marine Drive Co., which was promoted to construct a carriage drive on the top of the cliffs south of Douglas harbour, in emulation of the Great Orme at Llandudno which was popular at the time. The plan was to charge 2d a person and 6d for a carriage to enter the drive and enjoy spectacular sea views;

Douglas Head Suspension Bridge Co., which was supposed to build a suspension bridge across the harbour to link the upper part of Douglas with the Marine Drive, and build the Douglas Eiffel Tower in the harbour.

The three men were directors of all three companies and also shareholders. Dr Abbotts seems to crop up in about 1889 and pretty well disappears in 1893 as far as newspapers are concerned, although there are reports in 1895 of a Dr W. Abbotts publishing a medical book and recommending the Isle of Man as a place for asthmatics. He was the publisher of a medical magazine before the Isle of Man adventure and seems to have tried his hand as a company promoter from 1889–93. In February 1889 Dr Abbotts was involved with the promotion of a company called the London White Lead Manufacturing company, and then joined up with Darker Pitt, acting as chairman of companies where Darker Pitt was the managing director.[2]

Pearson[3] says that the Bridge company's prospectus was issued in April 1890, but notes that 30 per cent of the shares were bought by London-based investors and much of the rest by people based in Manchester and the North West more widely, very few were bought by Manx residents. The Bridge company entered into building contracts with Standard Contract and Debenture Corporation (SCDC) and land was acquired around Douglas Harbour.

The foundation stone for the Douglas Tower was laid on 24 October 1890. The *Manx Sun* of 25 October 1890 (p12) notes: 'A large quantity of property in and abutting Parade Street and Queen's Place has been acquired by the promoters at a cost of many thousands of pounds, and the work of demolition has been pushed on for some weeks by Messrs Carine and Chadwick with a numerous posse of workmen. A considerable area has been cleared, and a wonderful improvement has and will be wrought in this locality in many respects.'

However, just at this time the SCDC promoters were also working on Blackpool. A letter to the *Blackpool Gazette* on 14 November 1890 says there had been much talk about erecting a Blackpool Eiffel Tower, and suggested possible sites. Then an article in the *Gazette* on 28 November revealed the SCDC scheme. It said that the 'London syndicate' (SCDC used a London office address and no-one in Blackpool seems to have realised it was an Isle of Man company) had entered into negotiations with the company that ran the aquarium to buy the aquarium and the Beach Hotel on Central Beach for £60,000.[4]

The plan was to promote a new company, with capital of £150,000, which would then buy the site from SCDC. The agreement, according to Turner and Palmer,[5] was that SCDC would receive £95,000 from the yet-to-be floated Blackpool Tower Co. The *Blackpool Gazette* was enthusiastic: it said that a large number of the founder shares (with special residual rights to the profits) had already been taken up and the promoters were sure that the issue would be twice oversubscribed. The newspaper pointed out that a number of local dignitaries, including the mayor, John Bickerstaffe, but also Dr Cocker, the owner of the aquarium, had already signed up for shares. SCDC had already commissioned outline drawings of the Blackpool Tower, and were planning to submit these to the council for planning approval early in the following year.

A few days later the *Blackpool Gazette* (5 December 1890) reported that Mr Partington (a Blackpool businessman, the owner of the Palatine Hotel, who had been very active in the promotion so far) had had a further meeting with the SCDC directors in London and 'the scheme is being pushed ahead with the same amount of vigour and enterprise which characterised the preliminary negotiations.' The article said that the contract for the aquarium, menagerie and Beach Hotel had been signed and 'a considerable cash deposit paid'. They had decided not to issue the prospectus until early in the New Year, in light of the depression, but the paper said that the scheme had 'caught on' in Blackpool and it was thought Alderman Bickerstaffe and Alderman Cocker would be the local directors of the new company. Engineering firms would be asked to submit proposals for the construction.

The newspaper was enthusiastic about the despatch of the SCDC syndicate. However, the need for speed may well have been driven by the need for money. The subsequent liquidator of SCDC said only £730 of its capital had been subscribed; assuming that was so, it had no funds to carry out the Aquarium transactions. Even if SCDC paid only a deposit at this point, the newspaper described it as 'considerable'. The likelihood is that this money came from the two Douglas companies that were working on the Marine Drive and Douglas Tower.

SCDC would need to float the Blackpool Tower Co. quickly, in order to refund cash to the Isle of Man where building was taking place and would have to be paid for. In fact this was probably the high point of SCDC's existence. They had cash, thanks to the Douglas flotations, and Blackpool must have looked very promising, with a guaranteed £35,000 turn on the aquarium deal (millions in today's money) as soon as the Blackpool company was in business. As long as they could maintain momentum, the outlook was good. Christmas 1890 must have been a good one in the Darker Pitt household.

They held a meeting with interested parties at the Palatine Hotel and told them that they intended to complete the purchase of the Aquarium and the Beach Hotel very shortly. The *Blackpool Gazette* (27 Dec 1890) reported that there had been 'rumours of an adverse nature' circulating, and the promoters wanted to counter these. They also said that the share issue of the Blackpool Tower Co. would be underwritten by a London syndicate, so there was no doubt all the shares would be subscribed. The paper said: 'There is every indication that the Blackpool Tower will be a huge success and, at any rate, Mr Pitt and his colleagues are evidently losing no opportunity for rapidly pushing forward with this work as soon as a start can possibly be made.'

Despite this optimism, the new company was not launched for a while. The *Blackpool Gazette* ran a piece in February reassuring its readers that, if they had heard nothing, there was, nonetheless, great progress behind the scenes and the company would be registered shortly. And indeed it was: the certificate of incorporation is dated 23 February 1891, with a registered office in London.

The SCDC directors and some of the people working on the Isle of Man schemes also stopped in Blackpool for a banquet at the Palatine Hotel early in March. Dr Abbotts, described as chairman of the newly-formed Blackpool Tower Co., gave a speech praising Blackpool and talking about the opportunities for future progress. John Bickerstaffe replied, as mayor, saying he was confident that the Blackpool Tower would be a great success. Other speakers waxed lyrical about Blackpool soon being able to rival Brighton as the queen of watering places.

However, things were starting to go less well for SCDC in the Isle of Man – it was possibly running short of cash by this point, but disaster struck in Douglas when the digging of the foundations for the Douglas Tower undermined the gable end of the adjoining Royal Hotel in May 1891. The hotel owner immediately had all construction work stopped by court order, and caused the Suspension Bridge company to pay £1,500 into the court against repairs to the Royal Hotel. On the other hand, work seems to have progressed rapidly on the Marine Drive, and in July 1891 that company announced that two-thirds of the drive had been completed, and a part was opened to the public.

The detail of events in Blackpool becomes obscure at this point. The *Blackpool Gazette* (29 May 1891) said that the Tower Co. was to be launched imminently and that a board meeting was scheduled for the following week at which SCDC were intending to transfer the Aquarium and Beach Hotel formally to the Tower Co. But the next news (*Blackpool Gazette* 12 June 1891) is the confirmation of Maxwell and Tuke as architects of the tower, and then the Tower Co. initial public offering (IPO) is made in July. However, the prospectus shows John Bickerstaffe as chairman, with none of the original SCDC trio remaining on the board. The Blackpool *Gazette*, while reporting Bickerstaffe's comments as chairman, does not comment on the disappearance from the company of the previous chairman, Dr Abbotts, nor that of Darker Pitt.

It seems that Bickerstaffe went into the June board meeting as a director of the new company and came out as the chairman. Dr Abbotts, on the other hand, went in as chairman, and left without a seat on the board. It could be that this was a planned handover from the promoters to the operators of the company. The signature at that meeting of the agreement between SCDC and the Tower Company for the sale of the aquarium and the Beach Hotel and underwriting of the share issue underlines the nature of the meeting as marking a significant transition. It may also be that Bickerstaffe seized the moment to move the SCDC directors off the Tower board. In the light of subsequent events, it was a well-timed move.

The Initial Public Offering

The IPO was advertised on 27 July 1891, with subscriptions open only for a few days. The *Blackpool Gazette* ran the prospectus advertisement, and in the accompanying news item reported that £50,000 was already subscribed, with investors including no fewer than twelve members of parliament. The company was forecasting a dividend of 8 per cent, which the newspaper thought was reasonable given the commanding position the Tower would have, although 5–6 per cent might have been more in line with what other companies were paying at the time.

Beyond observing that the Tower would occupy a commanding position on the sea front between the two piers, and being enthusiastic about its prospects, the newspaper focused on the likely dividend, and discussed neither the detail of how this money was forecast to be created, nor the financing of the operation.

The prospectus was also published in the *Financial Times* on 27 July 1891 and gave more detail. It said that the site would cost £94,000 'a price that the directors consider is very favourable' and a current professional valuation put its market value at £98,535. It also specified that the buildings and fittings were expected to cost £120,000. The company was raising £150,000 in shares and said it would issue a debenture[6] for £85,000, thereby covering the initial cost.

The annual operating results were estimated as:

		£
Rents from shops, hotel, restaurants etc.	10,059	
Admissions to aquarium and entertainments	18,750	
(750,000 @ 6d)		
Admissions to Tower (500,000 @ 6d)	12,500	
		41,309
Less:		
Repairs, maintenance and establishment charges	9,000	
Depreciation	4,000	13,000
Profit		28,309
5 per cent on debenture	4,250	
8 per cent on 145,000 ordinary shares	11,600	15,850
Surplus		12,459

5,000 shares were designated as founders' shares and would qualify for half of the surplus.

In fact the profit forecast was not that far out in terms of the actual outturn once the Tower was built. This forecast assumed, however, that the Tower Co. would rent out its buildings and not operate entertainments itself, and that was ultimately not the case. In the event the company did run bars, restaurants and entertainment and consequently had much higher turnover and expenses. In the first ten years of operation the company generated an after-tax profit of between £20,000 and £30,000 a year, except in 1894, the year it opened, when the profit was smaller.

The balance sheet on the other hand looks overly optimistic with the benefit of hindsight. Eventually the land and buildings, fixture and fittings cost about £50,000 more than the prospectus estimated (more than 40 per cent).[7] The prospectus was also the first time there had been any mention of the debenture. At the June board meeting, the directors had agreed Maxwell and Tuke's proposals at £120,000. Had the SCDC significantly underestimated the construction cost previously, and given Bickerstaffe a lever to get rid of them as a consequence? Had the board, given Bickerstaffe's track record, gone for the most expensive quotation and had to come up with a way of meeting a funding gap? Unfortunately no private correspondence survives, nor any board minutes for the period. Bickerstaffe later made it abundantly clear that funding was a major problem throughout the subsequent construction period.

The prospectus clearly states that SCDC was to absorb all the costs of the IPO and guarantee the whole of the share capital. However, in the autumn of 1891 creditors of the Marine Drive and Suspension Bridge companies, as well as SCDC, started to show up in the Isle of Man courts. In December the *Blackpool Gazette* ran a piece reporting a 'rumour' that a meeting had taken place between the SCDC directors and those of the Tower to settle the contract for the acquisition of the aquarium. The newspaper reported that SCDC had failed to meet its obligations under the contract, and the Tower Co. was invoking a penalty clause. A week later the Tower Co. announced that it had settled with SCDC – for £72,800 instead of £94,000, and had taken possession of Dr Cocker's aquarium, menagerie and Beach Hotel.

The nature of the failure was not specified, but it is evident that SCDC was unable to meet its guarantee of the issue of Tower shares. Getting a reduction of £21,200 was seen as a significant coup on Bickerstaffe's part, meaning that the Tower Co. had acquired its site at well below market price. As the newspaper pointed out, the SCDC directors were no longer on the board of the Tower Co., and had no role to play in the further life of that company. The cut in price was John Bickerstaffe's parting gift to SCDC as he took control of the whole operation.

The Isle of Man

In January 1892 SCDC petitioned the Isle of Man court for a winding up order, and in March 1892 this was made compulsory. This caused problems for the Marine Drive and Suspension Bridge companies, which had had contracts with SCDC and much of whose money had been given to SCDC. The Marine Drive shareholders commissioned an accountant's report on the company. This noted that the project was 'three-quarters or four-fifths' completed and, at a meeting in Manchester in January 1892, the shareholders agreed to raise more money to complete the project.

The outcome for the Suspension Bridge Co. was less positive. In January 1892 there were reports in the papers of work being restarted on the Tower site, but in April 1892 a compulsory winding up order was made for this company as well, and the liquidator's report as at 31 January 1893 (*Isle of Man Times* 18 February 1893) showed a deficiency of £63,278. This was the end of the Douglas Eiffel Tower.

The Douglas Head Marine Drive Co. was, however, successful. Having appointed new directors, including a Dr Farrell from the Isle of Man, the company paid off the outstanding claims, was freed of its ties to SCDC as a result of the latter's failure, and set about completing the project on its own. It advanced less rapidly than it might because of the tightness of funds, but the Marine Drive was fully open by May 1895. Nonetheless profits were disappointing, with the directors reporting at the end of the season that the Drive was suffering as a result of the popularity of an electric tram going to the north from Douglas to Laxey.

The board thought there should be an electric tram to serve the Marine Drive to the south of the town. They decided to float another company, the Douglas Southern Electric Tramways Co., which would build and operate the tram, and pay the Marine Drive Co. a royalty. This was done, and the tramway opened successfully in 1896 and made the Marine Drive Co. profitable.

A recent history of the Douglas Marine Drive by George Hobbs[8] says that the tramway along the marine drive continued to function until 1939 but activity was suspended with the start of the Second World War and never restarted. One of the original tramcars can still be found at the Crich Tram Museum in Derbyshire (not far from Sheffield). He comments that the service eventually suffered from competition from buses. The marine drive is no longer open to vehicles along the whole of its length, but is accessible as part of a coastal path around the island. The Laxey tramway still operates, however, and goes on to Snaefell (the highest point on the Isle of Man).

Darker Pitt

The reaction in the Isle of Man press to the demise of SCDC and the Douglas Tower project was harsh. One article ('A Joint Stock Utopia' *Manx Sun* 21 May 1892) described SCDC as 'English speculators', suggesting the use of an Isle of Man Co. was a sham, as the management was based in London. It noted that it was much cheaper to set up the Isle of Man Co. than it would have been to register in London. The judge who made the winding up order commented that SCDC was abusing Isle of Man law. The *Isle of Man Examiner* (21 May 1892) did an analysis of SCDC's receipts and expenditure. This suggested that SCDC had received £15,000 from the Blackpool Tower Co. but spent £18,000 on the venture. It had received £23,000 from the Marine Drive Co. but spent £35,000, leaving the Douglas Suspension Bridge and Tower as the loser, having paid in £31,000 to SCDC but receiving only £10,000.

While SCDC was falling apart, the indefatigable Darker Pitt was working on a new scheme in Scarborough. There, as the London and General Contract Co. (LGCC), he was attempting to promote the construction of Scarborough Winter Gardens, based on options issued in November 1891 to acquire property at King's Cliffe. A new company was to be floated, the Scarborough Winter Gardens Co., and LGCC was to guarantee all the costs of the share issue. LGCC was to buy the land for £25,000 and sell it to the new company for £31,900 (*Isle of Man Times* 7 March 1893).

The paper notes that Dr Abbotts and F. A. Darlington were also directors of LGCC. It reports that Darker Pitt had been made bankrupt in 1885. He had started his career as a financial agency in Manchester in 1877. His early ventures included the Manchester Domestic Servants' Registry Association, followed by the Bank of Wales, the Bank of Oldham and then the Staffordshire Union Bank and the National Syndicate Trust. He seems then to have turned to seaside resorts and the Isle of Man Tramway Co., which the newspaper says also failed. Despite this track record, the *Financial Times* articles of February 1899 show that he was still promoting the formation of public companies and selling land and money-making schemes to them at the end of the decade.

4

BUILDING THE BLACKPOOL TOWER

1891 was the year in which the Blackpool Tower Co. was floated on the Manchester stock exchange and, by the end of the year, planning permission had been given, the aquarium, menagerie and Beach Hotel had been passed to the new company and the foundation stone had been laid with great ceremony. It would, though, be another three years before it opened for business, and John Bickerstaffe would be constantly short of finance and facing a falling share price.

The promoters had run a competition for the design of the Tower, and the contract had been awarded to Maxwell and Tuke, a Manchester firm. Their design was given a full page spread in the *Blackpool Gazette* in June 1891, after it had been given planning permission. The *Blackpool Gazette* (12 June 1891) quoted a description of the design by the London correspondent of the *Manchester Guardian*:

I have today seen the accepted plans for the Blackpool Tower. It promises to be a handsome structure. The base is a substantial building of two storeys, with a long frontage to the esplanade. The ground floor front is designed to be let as shops, while the interior forms a circus or entertainment theatre. Above this the first floor is almost entirely occupied by a banqueting or ballroom of large dimensions. From the centre of this building of brick and stone there rises in light open ironwork the tower itself to a height of 460ft. The design is very similar in outward appearance to the famous Parisian Tower, the airy and graceful effect, which is perhaps the most wonderful feature of that colossal structure, being excellently reproduced.

Now all that was needed was to start building, and for that money was required. The Blackpool Tower Co. made its initial public offering (IPO) in July, with John Bickerstaffe at the helm. People applying for £1 ordinary shares were asked to pay 1s[1] on application (5 per cent of the nominal value). Those to whom shares were allocated would then have to pay a further 4s (20 per cent) on allotment, and the balance in three instalments of 5s (25 per cent each).

Nowadays people applying for shares in an IPO usually have to put up the full price, but in the nineteenth century and for part of the twentieth century it was normal to claim the full subscription in instalments. Indeed, it was possible for the bulk of the nominal amount to remain outstanding ('at call') to be received only if the company needed the cash. This could be abused because a company could have (say) £100,000 nominal capital subscribed, while showing an 'asset' of £80,000 shares at call – in other words only 20 per cent of the nominal capital had actually been paid to the company.

This was not the case for the Tower Co. The *Gazette* announced on 7 August 1891 that the full capital of £150,000 had been applied for, and the board had met in London to allocate the shares. The article says nothing about the debenture loan which had also been on offer in the IPO prospectus.

The next public event was the laying of the foundation stone. This took place on 25 September 1891, with Blackpool decked out with bunting for the occasion. The *Gazette* reports (2 October 1891) that 'the concourse of people on the Promenade during the progress of the procession was certainly one of the largest ever witnessed in the town, and the enterprise and public spirit of the directors of the Tower Co. in making their arrangements on so lavish a scale undoubtedly deserves the fullest recognition.'

The Manchester Times reported (2 October 1891) that at 2 p.m. a procession left the Imperial Hotel and drove along the greater part of the promenade. It notes that the procession included the mayors of Clitheroe, Mossley, Kendall, Newcastle-under-Lyme, Chorley, Stafford, Stalybridge, Heywood, Crewe, Bacup, Burslem, Rawtenstall, Dewsbury, Darwen, Wakefield, Accrington, Southport, Ashton-under-Lyme, Macclesfield, Burton on Trent, Warrington, Dudley, Bury, Rochdale, Halifax, Huddersfield, Preston, Blackburn, Oldham, Hull and Salford.

It is not difficult to imagine that Bickerstaffe had invited, as mayor of Blackpool,[2] all the mayors of all the towns of any size in Lancashire and the neighbouring counties. Their presence would presumably have guaranteed coverage in the local newspapers across the region and the maximum impact on potential future customers. It would also have had the effect of reassuring people who had already invested in the Tower Co., supporting the share price, and encouraging further investment. The coverage in *The Manchester Times* went into great detail on the proposed building, explaining that the surrounding complex would include a circus, aquarium, balconies, shops and cafes, occupying a site of some 6,000 square yards.

The foundation stone was laid by Sir Matthew White Ridley, the member of Parliament for Blackpool (and a shareholder in the company). John Bickerstaffe opened proceedings, as Mayor, Mr Tuke, the architect, handed Sir Matthew a silver trowel, and Dr Abbotts, as chairman of the SCDC but no longer of the Tower, provided an ivory mallet. After that a band played, photographs were taken, and eventually the 150 official guests returned to the Imperial Hotel for a banquet and further speeches. The paper says 'weather of the most magnificent description favoured the festivities'.

The Liquor Licence

On the face of it, all was going very well. The initial capital had theoretically been raised – albeit with a credit risk:[3] given that only 5 per cent was paid on application and the rest would follow over time. The foundation stone had been laid, with maximum publicity, and all that remained was to start building.

However, the company had meantime suffered a curious legal set-back. The site on which the Tower was to be built was occupied by the Aquarium/Menagerie and the Beach Hotel. Both of these premises had liquor licences, and could sell alcohol to their customers. However, they were both to be knocked down, and so the Tower Co. asked, in August, for the licences to be transferred to its yet-to-be built bars. The magistrates refused.

Although the business model was based on people paying to go up the Tower, the complex included different attractions as well as restaurants, cafes and bars, so that more money could be made from those attracted in by the Tower. Sales of alcoholic beverages usually are priced to provide a high profit margin, but their absence in the cafes and restaurants would also detract from those businesses, causing customers to go elsewhere. A liquor licence was an essential to maximise the profitability of the Tower.

The licensing system at that time operated on a year-to-year basis. The license to sell alcohol was granted by the local magistrates' bench. It was personal to the bar manager, related to specific rooms and had to be renewed each year. People who kept an unruly house would find that their application to renew their licence was opposed by the police, so the system was used in a very direct way as a means of keeping order. The annual renewal of licences was not a formality.

In the case of the Beach Hotel and the Aquarium, the company was represented in court by Thomas Smethurst, its Manchester-based auditor. Professional ethics would not allow the company auditor to do that today, but John Bickerstaffe was a justice of the peace and sat on the licensing bench. He was not presiding for this case, but no doubt he would have found it embarrassing to apply in person, so Smethurst represented the company. The presiding magistrate, however, did not go along with the proposal. He said that he understood the problem, and did not wish to oppose a license being granted to the Tower Co. eventually, but he could not give a license to operate bars in a building that did not exist.

The decision caused consternation in the Tower Co. Were they supposed to erect the tower and buildings at great expense and not know whether they would eventually be able to sell alcohol? It should not be forgotten that the foundation of the Bickerstaffe fortune had been the sale of liquor at the Wellington Hotel, and liquor was also an important income stream on the paddle steamers. The laying of the foundation stone was imminent.

The *Blackpool Gazette* (4 September 1891) reported on a board meeting where the directors decided 'not a brick shall be removed from its present position (in the existing buildings) until the provisional license had been obtained.' The paper added that if the license was refused, work scheduled for the winter would be put back a year, at considerable cost to those who would have been employed, and to the Tower Co. Apparently convinced that the magistrates' bench would relent when it reconvened on 28 September, the directors fixed on 25 September to lay the foundation stone.

The *Gazette* reported in its 2 October issue not only the laying of the foundation stone, but also the second refusal of the magistrates to allow the licenses of the Beach Hotel and the Aquarium to be transferred. The paper quotes a magistrate, Mr E. Birley, that the application would be of no avail unless the buildings were completed or in course of completion. It says the magistrates were unanimous in rejecting the application. The newspaper speculates that it might be possible to start work on the northern part of the new buildings without disturbing the existing ones, and apply for a transfer of the license the following year. In the event, the company did indeed preserve the original buildings as long as possible and construct the Tower around them.

However, the incident undoubtedly created negative publicity and probably affected the secondary market for Tower Co. shares. Although a lot of press attention was paid to the initial public offering, most trading on stock exchanges relates to the secondary market. Once people have bought shares in the IPO of a listed company, they can sell the shares on to anyone who wants to buy them – this is the secondary market. The conventional wisdom is that a buyer on the stock exchange will be willing to pay an amount that equates to the cash flows, adjusted for the time value of money,[4] that the buyer expects to receive. Saying that the Tower might be delayed for a year would immediately cause the market price of the shares to drop because the eventual dividends would be that much further away.

At this particular point there was also a significant risk that people who had subscribed for shares but not yet paid the instalments would fail to pay the balance. If in the secondary market a fully-paid Tower ordinary share was selling for £1 or more, initial subscribers would be happy. However, if the price in the secondary market dropped below £1, subscribers would start to get unhappy. Worse, if someone had been allotted shares and paid a total of 5s, with another 15s to pay in instalments, once the secondary market price dropped to less than 15s, it would be cheaper to buy in the market and forfeit the original shares.

On 9 October the *Gazette* published a letter from Maxwell and Tuke, the architects, which said that stories of the Tower being delayed had been put about to injure the company. The letter points out that Mr Birley, the magistrate, had specified that the refusal to license new premises was purely on technical grounds, and the press should not assume the bench had the intention of ultimately refusing a license for the Tower. The letter assured people that the company had decided to start erecting the tower at once. They expected work to start before the end of October, and that the greater part of the Tower would be complete before the following July. The company had renewed the licenses for the Beach Hotel and the Aquarium, and these would remain in operation.

It seems that the architects were a little optimistic in their forecast. In December the *Gazette* was reporting that some demolition was expected the following week, and contractors had been appointed to construct the foundations. December saw a settlement with Standard Contract and Debenture Corporation (SCDC), as discussed in Chapter Three.

The SCDC had contracted to meet the whole of the costs of the share issue up to allotment, and to guarantee the share capital. The company said the shares had been fully subscribed, but it may be that some people who were allotted shares did not take them up. SCDC was short of money by December 1891 and was probably asked to make good its guarantee and failed to do so. John Bickerstaffe's connections with the Isle of Man were good – steamers from the South Jetty ran trips there regularly, as the Isle of Man Steam Packet Co. did in the opposite direction. Bickerstaffe may well have heard of SCDC's growing difficulties in the island.

The *Gazette* of 4 December talks about the directors invoking a penalty clause, but is no more explicit than that. It notes that this is a good gain for the shareholders and adds: 'If they are victims of circumstance, the Standard Contract and Debenture Corporation are undoubtedly to be sympathised with, for the original conception of the scheme was due to them, and it is to their pluck and perseverance that Blackpool will own the great attraction that the Eiffel Tower is expected to be.'

Construction Starts

In any event, the Tower Co. completed the purchase of the Beach Hotel and the Aquarium and was able to start work. The idea that any part of the new complex would be finished for the summer of 1892 was optimistic, and even in November 1892 the *Gazette* was reporting only that 800 tonnes of ironwork had been erected and the legs were standing at 55 feet. It said the foundations for the shops and entrance on the north-east corner of the building had been laid, and three of the 'keep' walls around the tower had been constructed to a height of 30 feet.

The Tower Co. held its first annual shareholders meeting in December 1892, and the information provided in the accounts, as discussed in the newspaper, show that the company's capital position was less healthy than might have been thought. The

Gazette (14 December 1892) reported that its share capital as at 31 October 1892 was:

Class	Issued	Paid-up
	£	£
Ordinary shares	76,877	62,081
Founders shares	5,000	4,665
6 per cent preference shares	21,821	5,089
Total	103,698	71,835

The newspaper reported the company's fixed assets as being:

	£
Site	60,000
Paid to SCDC	12,800
Stamping and other share costs	604
Preliminary expenses	1,662
Construction	16,138
Alterations, fittings per cent equipment	1,377
Livestock (aquarium/menagerie)	4,000
Development account	879
Total	97,460

The newspaper noted (approvingly) that, despite the building work, the Beach Hotel and the Aquarium had between them generated a profit of £2,342 which had enabled the company to pay a preference dividend and interest on the mortgage and still leave a surplus of £644. The newspaper did not comment on the fact that the subscribed share capital was less than the £150,000 it reported as having been achieved at the time of the IPO. No preference shares were offered in the IPO, and yet some had subsequently been issued. The newspaper did not ask how the company was going to fund the estimated £100,000 still required to complete the buildings.

In fact, on the figures published in the *Gazette*, the company's assets exceed its paid up capital by some £26,000. How was that achieved? British companies were not required to file an annual balance sheet with Companies House until 1907, and so only the newspaper account exists. However, the newspaper referred to paying interest on a mortgage, and information from later years shows that the company had received £30,000 from Blackpool Corporation,[5] by way of a mortgage.

It is fairly clear that, despite the optimistic reports in August 1891, not all the shares had been subscribed, SCDC had not met their guarantee, and John Bickerstaffe had been forced to go looking for money. He had issued preference shares (while these are shares, and the holders receive a dividend, but the securities resemble debt in that this is a fixed return, and is paid as a priority ahead of any dividend on ordinary shares). He had also negotiated a mortgage with the Blackpool Corporation.

The shareholders' meeting took place at the Prince of Wales Hotel. Alderman Bickerstaffe told the meeting that the directors met the shareholders 'with far lighter hearts than they were able to some time ago.' He claimed that the good profits earned from the Beach Hotel and the Aquarium were an indication of how much more they would earn when the Tower was in use. He clarified that the directors had been authorised to issue £40,000 of 6 per cent preference shares, which had been offered to existing ordinary shareholders, but only just over half had so far been taken up. He added that he hoped shareholders would take advantage of what was 'a perfectly safe investment', but that they would be offered to the general public if not taken up.

Three years later, at the 1895 annual meeting, Bickerstaffe referred back to this one, saying 'it required a little nerve in order to lay before them the financial statement.' At the 1896 meeting he went so far as to say that the company would have been bankrupt but for the preference shares. He described the company as being 'on a lee shore' at the end of 1891. They had paid about

£73,000 for the land ... and there was only about £71,000 of ordinary capital subscribed. They had practically nothing with which to commence the Tower and buildings.' He added that at the beginning of 1892 that they had no capital, they were in financial difficulties, their shares were down at about eleven shillings.

At the 1892 meeting the manager of the construction company said that they aimed to have the work complete for the season of 1893, but that was not to be. A ceremony to celebrate the completion of the tower was not held until October 1893. Sadly neither Mr Maxwell nor Mr Tuke, the architects, had lived long enough to see the tower completed. The work had taken two years, and had not involved any fatalities among the workers (although one worker had fallen to his death, but since this had occurred during the breakfast break, it was not considered to have happened during construction!).

In 1893 the Tower Co. hosted officials from the Eiffel Tower. The *Gazette* reported (30 March 1893) that the Eiffel Tower had cost £200,400, but after three years of operation the profits had been £282,000. The original capital had been refunded to shareholders and over £80,000 on top of that. The newspaper comments: 'We are not so sanguine as to anticipate that the Blackpool Tower will pay for itself, and earn a substantial sum in addition, within the short space of three years, but there is every reason to believe that with good management the Tower Co. will pay good, not to say handsome, dividends to those who have invested in it.' The *Gazette* was a staunch supporter of the Tower project, and it is not hard to see the invitation to the Eiffel Tower management as emanating from Bickerstaffe with the intention of bolstering the shares.

The 1893 annual shareholders' meeting was not held until the end of the year. The *Gazette* was not as forthcoming on the detail of the financial statements as the previous year, but it was clear that the trading result had been poorer – John Bickerstaffe explained that part of the premises had not been available as a result of the building work. He observed that the company had 'passed through very troublous waters.' He added that they had almost been on their beam ends on a lee shore, but, thanks to a good ship, which was well-manned, they had been able to beat to windward and arrive in a safe harbour without even the loss of a spar or a stitch of canvas.

He added that the lifts would shortly be operational in the tower and they would complete the remaining buildings during 1894. There would be a circus, which the directors had decided should be run directly by the company, as opposed to letting the space to a circus company. He noted that the company had benefited from the experience of working on the north buildings to order the terracotta facing tiles early, because these had previously caused a great delay in construction. Asked by a shareholder if the company had enough money to complete the buildings, the chairman said: 'When we have issued the debenture capital we shall have enough.'

In his main address Bickerstaffe had observed that people were saying that once the novelty of the tower had worn off, revenues would drop dramatically. He pointed out that the complex would have a number of different attractions and was not wholly dependent on the tower.

One of the features of the 1893 meeting was that there was a lot of discussion of the auditor's remuneration. A shareholder question elicited the information that the auditor's fee was £40 (included in development expenses). Another thought this was excessive and the fee should be determined by the shareholders, and fixed in advance. Bickerstaffe countered that until the company had settled down into its expected pattern of operations, it was difficult to determine a reasonable fee. As regards 1893 he was convinced that the cost of the clerks sent by Mr Smethurst was not even covered by that fee. Eventually the meeting reappointed Thomas Smethurst, and left it to the directors to determine the 1894 fee.

In fact Thomas Smethurst was no ordinary auditor. He built up a very significant practice, based on Manchester, and eventually sold the firm to what is now Ernst & Young (or EY). Jones[6] includes a photograph of Smethurst's office in his book. He says that Smethurst was born in Middleton and had significant clients there, but his main clients were Manchester-based, and he lived in Lytham on the Fylde coast and also built up a clientele which included theatres and music hall performers. He served a term as lord mayor of Manchester from 1916 to 1918. Smethurst was knighted (KBE) in 1920 in the context of a series of civilian honours related to the First World War. His citation was as chairman of the Manchester War Savings Committee.

He was made Justice of the Peace in 1928, when the *Gazette* reported that he had been a banker before moving in to accountancy. There is little doubt that Smethurst was closely involved with Bickerstaffe and his financial advice may have been crucial in keeping the Tower Co. afloat in the difficult 1891–94 construction years.

His firm was eventually merged with that of Whinney Smith and Murray. Jones (p164) says that the firm wanted to establish a Manchester base to service their client Dunlop. 'A merger with Smethurst had the advantage of providing a nucleus of local clients, a respected name and an introduction to the city's commercial world'. The firm became Whinney Smethurst from 1928.

Today the world of international audit is dominated by four very large firms. The development of these firms has typically been through merger between British and American firms, which have then attracted national firms in all parts of the world to join them. Ernst & Young is a case in point. Whinney Smith and Murray can trace their UK constituent firms back to about 1840, and by the end of the century, as the role of accountancy firms became more defined and codified, they emerged as one of the larger UK firms, with strengths in London and Scotland.

To service their clients they developed regional offices, either by taking in regional firms such as Smethurst's, or starting new offices. In the second half of the twentieth century, as their clients spread their activities overseas, the firms needed to follow them, and started to merge with US firms that had followed a similar pattern of development. Whinney Smith and Murray merged with Ernst and Ernst in the US, becoming Ernst & Whinney in 1979. In a further consolidation of the profession, they were joined in 1989 by Arthur Young, becoming Ernst & Young (now 'EY').

Open for Business

The Tower finally opened for business in May 1894. Although great efforts had been made to publicise the laying of the foundation stone in 1891, the Tower had no grand opening. The reason for this was simple: it was not ready! The holiday season in the UK is short, especially in the north, and if the June–August peak is missed, probably 90 per cent of annual sales are lost. It was imperative both for the company's finances and the share price, that the company was open for business in the 1894 season, and ideally should even make enough money to pay a dividend. Consequently, although building and fitting out was still going on, Bickerstaffe opted to open bits of the business as soon as this was feasible, and the main attractions opened progressively during the summer.

The Tower opened in early May, with the aquarium and some form of entertainment also being available. The *Gazette* reported that 3,000 people ascended the Tower on the first day alone – that should have yielded £75 at 6d per person. The newspaper said that 'the patronage of the aquatic and variety entertainment has been equally extensive'. The circus opened at the end of May, and much was made in the newspapers of the water feature – the floor of the circus could be withdrawn to reveal a tank, in which swimming and diving displays were given as part of the show. However, the ballroom (the chairman refers to this as the Assembly Hall at this point) did not open until August, and a liquor licence was not given until then. The shops were not finished and indeed work was still going on after the end of the season.

Despite the fact that the complex was now attracting visitors, at the end of September the £1 ordinary shares were trading at only 17s, even if the preference shares were changing hands at face value. In November the company published its accounts, showing a profit of £12,389, out of which the directors planned to pay a dividend of 4 per cent to ordinary shareholders, as well as paying the 6 per cent due on the preference shares.

The *Gazette* of 16 November 1894 provided the following figures:

Financing	£
Ordinary shares	91,299
Founders' shares	4,750
Preference shares	39,149
Total equity:	99,998
Debenture	68,650
Blackpool Corporation mortgage	30,000
Total	198,648

Assets	£
Land	73,404
Construction	141,778
Plant, fixtures and fittings	13,234
Livestock	5,000
Formation and preliminary expenses	2,910
Development expenses	2,193
Bank	6,227
Total	244,746

The newspaper's figures presumably omit some liabilities, since they show financing that is £46,000 less than the company's assets. This could well be amounts due on the construction, and if so, begs the question of how Bickerstaffe was going to be able to pay this and the dividends. However, at the annual general meeting, he asked for approval of the issue of a 'B' debenture of £30,000.

He said that the total cost of the complex was going to rise to £280,000, and that this was as a result of extending the work and improving things. He cited as an example a decision to rebuild the existing aquarium in line with the new building around it. He said shop rents would increase the following year, as many had been unfinished. The fact that the building had not been completed could be put down to delays in delivery of building materials, especially the terracotta tiles. He promised the building would be complete for the following season.

Bickerstaffe referred to the Tower as 'one of the finest specimens of engineering work in the country'. He thanked shareholders for their patience and confidence, and the financial support they had given the directors. He added: 'You know that the erection of this gigantic structure could not have been accomplished without a great amount of tact, ability, and self-sacrifice and, shall I say, backbone on the part of your board of management.' He also noted with pleasure that the chairman of the North Pier Co. had welcomed the Tower, and that the published results of the other local companies showed that everyone had had a good year, which implied that the Tower added to the level of business in the resort, rather than taking business away from others.

However, even a year later, at the 1895 annual meeting the chairman said that the building work was not complete, and asked the shareholders for permission to increase the capital of the company.

A Close-Run Thing

The Blackpool Tower Co. was profitable, and paid a dividend, from the first year that it was open for business, and it continued to be a profitable business until it was taken over by EMI in 1966 (independent figures are not available after that date). However, it had very nearly failed. At the 1896 annual meeting John Bickerstaffe said he believed that when the buildings were completed, they would achieve a great success (and his confidence was shown by the great amount of money he had invested in it). He believed it would prove to be one of the best paying companies in Blackpool, if only they could get sufficient money to invest in the buildings. At the end of 1892 the company would have gone into liquidation if the shareholders had not subscribed for the preference shares.

The first figures published by the company that have survived in the company archive to the present day are for the 1897 balance sheet numbers. The tables below show the 1897 actual figures against the 1891 prospectus:

Financing	30 Sept 1897	Prospectus
	£	£
Ordinary share capital	105,000	145,000
Founders shares	4,785	5,000
Preference shares	40,000	-
Equity sub-total	149,785	150,000
A Debenture (1894, 1895)	70,000	85,000
B Debenture (1895)	30,000	-
C Debenture (1896)	20,000	-
Mortgage Blackpool Corporation	30,000	-
Debt sub-total	150,000	85,000
Total Financing	299,785	235,000

Assets		
Property	74,605	94,000
Buildings	189,826	120,000
Plant per cent Machinery	15,888	-
Furniture and Fittings	11,993	-
Stock (bars, aquarium etc.)	5,814	-
Total	298,126	214,000

In effect a project that had originally been mooted as costing £150,000 had ended up requiring a £300,000 investment. Of course, cost over-runs remain to this day a 'normal' part of large construction projects. In this case it is quite likely that Darker Pitt and his Standard Contract and Debenture Corporation deliberately underestimated the cost to enhance the feasibility of their proposal. The estimated capital required increased from £150,000 at the beginning of 1891 to £235,000 at the time of the flotation of the Tower Co. However there was after that a net overrun of more than 25 per cent. This was made up (in round terms) as follows:

	£
Tower building	70,000
Plant & machinery	16,000
Fixtures and fittings	12,000
Stock	6,000
Saving on property	-20,000
Net	84,000

There is no information about what specifically caused the cost increases, but we do know that John Bickerstaffe believed in high quality and it is likely that this was a factor, as well as probably changing the specification as the building proceeded. There was also the issue of having to work around the Beach Hotel and Aquarium rather than to demolish them on day one of construction.

One half of Bickerstaffe's nightmare was therefore that the construction was more expensive by some distance than had been anticipated. The other half was that funding was nowhere near as good as expected. The 1891 data shows that of the anticipated £145,000 ordinary shares, only £77,000 had been subscribed for, of which only £62,000 had been received. This was in a context where the company was supposed to pay £94,000 to Standard Contract and Debenture Corporation for the land. Bickerstaffe's solution was in three parts: (1) obtain a mortgage from Blackpool Corporation for £30,000; (2) apply a penalty clause in the Standard Contract and Debenture Corporation's contract to reduce their fee by £20,000, and (3) issue preference shares (eventually reaching £40,000). A combination of these three kept the company going at the end of 1891 and enabled it to start construction. This seems to have been the most serious financing crisis, although the Company was going to have financing problems up to 1897.

At the 1892 annual meeting, Mr Heenan, the overall contractor for the construction, told shareholders that he had agreed to have 25 per cent of his contract paid in ordinary shares, and had pledged not to sell them until the Tower was operational. He said he would be due 15,000 shares in all. Between the 1891 meeting and the 1897 meeting ordinary shares increased from 77,000 to 105,000, and clearly part of this increase came from the company using the shares as cash, another Bickerstaffe financing manoeuvre that is also alive and well in the twenty-first century.

The Tower Co. managed apparently to keep building without further finance until it started issuing its 'A' debenture in 1894. Bickerstaffe took a decision to pay a dividend as early as possible to ordinary shareholders, while then borrowing more money to complete the buildings. In fact the company issued £120,000 of debentures between 1894 and 1896. It may conceivably have used short term bank borrowing in 1893 and 1894 and repaid that with the debentures issued at a more favourable rate once the Tower was open. The newspaper reports of the annual meetings do not provide detail on this.

At future shareholder meetings, John Bickerstaffe often referred back to this period as one of the most difficult in his life. At the 1920 general meeting Bickerstaffe said they had had their difficulties, as his friend Sir Thomas Smethurst would remember, in the early days of the company. They had had an uphill fight at that time, and he could tell them he would not like – in fact he could not do it now – to go through the first two years' existence of the Tower again. It was in the balance at one time whether they went into liquidation or not, but they had stuck to their guns. He had invested money which he could ill afford at that time in order to create confidence (*Blackpool Gazette* 21 December 1920).

5

DEVELOPMENT AND CONSOLIDATION

The financing, construction and opening of the Blackpool Tower was a major achievement, due entirely to the determination of John Bickerstaffe, and the conviction of his team that the Tower would be profitable. The opponents and pessimists had said that the Tower would be a five minute wonder: it would attract the curious but once they had ascended, there would be no more customers. Others said it would just draw customers away from the other attractions. Bickerstaffe on the other hand believed that not only would it remain a popular attraction, but that it would bring new holidaymakers to Blackpool.

Bickerstaffe was right – the company made a profit every year of its life as an independent operation.[1] Those shareholders who had held their nerve were amply rewarded – and showed their gratitude to John Bickerstaffe by presenting him in 1897 with a silver replica of the Tower. The silver model was ultimately given by him to the company and can be seen on display in the Tower today.

Having created a successful business, the next question was whether to concentrate on running that business, or to expand. Bickerstaffe's energy and vision were such that expanding the business was the only choice, but keeping the business constantly up to date with changes in entertainment was also a major concern. Films started to be shown to paying audiences in London in 1896, and by 1897 the Tower Co. was able to show what Brian Hornsey[2] calls 'a brief and flickering film entitled "The Queen of the North"' in the Tower Pavilion (later to be the Ballroom).

Initially films were shown in theatres and pavilions as a novelty within a larger entertainment by live performers, although Hornsey says that people also erected large tents on the beach specifically to screen films. He cites the creation in 1906 of the 'Collosseum' (a building removed from Raikes Hall Gardens and reused as a cinema) as the first independent full time cinema.

1897 was notable for the Tower Co. in a less desirable way – the Tower caught fire. Fortunately it was the upper part of the Tower itself that was damaged and not so much the buildings around its base, and no-one was hurt. Bickerstaffe later recounted to the 1897 shareholders' meeting (*Blackpool Gazette & News* 26 October 1897) that he had returned to Blackpool from London by train, and when getting off the train towards midnight on 22 July had been told by the station staff that the Tower was on fire. Using a maritime analogy he said there was nothing worse than a fire at sea, but he had been relieved to discover that the fire was only in the rigging, and not in the hold. He noted that it was marvellous that so little damage had been done, and congratulated the police, fire service and his own staff.

However, the lifts to get to the top of the tower were out of action for the rest of the season. This meant that they had lost the 6d per person that was charged to use the lift, and they believed that fewer people entered the complex, so door receipts (also 6d per person) were down. Some shareholders queried why the lifts had not been replaced more quickly. Bickerstaffe replied that the directors could have done that, but they had learned from the experience of running the lifts and had decided to make significant improvements.

The counterbalances of the lifts had fallen through the roof of the north-east leg during the fire and damaged the circus. Bill Curtis[2] says that the counterweight landed in a circus box and it was too complicated to remove it, so it was left there and the box was boarded in and concealed. Once the new lifts were in place, any falling counterweight would drop into sand or wood. There would be no more fires at the top of the Tower – there would be nothing there that could burn.

The sales in 1897 were nearly 10 per cent down on the previous year, as a result of the fire, and expenses were up, partly as a result of repairing the effects of the fire, and partly, as Bickerstaffe explained, that with growing competition they had had to engage more expensive performers to continue to attract holidaymakers. The result was that the dividend was to be reduced by about 20 per cent. Bickerstaffe had been concerned before the meeting that shareholders would be angry about this.

The meeting was held in the Tower Circus, and the chairman had arranged that Wallace, a lion from the menagerie, should be available in a mobile cage, to be brought in as a diversion if the meeting got out of hand – in the event the shareholders did not need to be thus tamed. As the *Gazette* put it:

> The shareholders, assembled on a Saturday afternoon in the Circus, were as quiet as the proverbial lambs. There was very little grumbling and a harmonious meeting passed off without any occasion for the introduction of Wallace, the finest lion the company possesses.

That could have been among the more memorable of company annual general meetings had things gone differently.

Whether motivated by the improvements to the Tower made as a result of fire, or as a result of increased competition (the Winter Gardens had created a new ballroom, the Empress Ballroom, and the Alhambra was being constructed next door to the Tower), the company soon after undertook a major refurbishment of the buildings. According to Vanessa Toulmin[4] the room that occupied the space above the café and restaurant, known as the Tower Pavilion, was a general purpose room used for occasional screening of films during the day and for dances in the evening.

Over the winter of (1898–99), Bickerstaffe engaged Frank Matcham, the leading theatre designer of the period, to remodel the pavilion as a ballroom, giving it the décor that it still has today, as well as the circus and the Tower restaurant. To finance this, the company had issued 35,000 new ordinary shares – which were this time sold with no difficulty and including a premium above their face value.

The upgrading of the premises started in 1898 with improvements to the roof gardens and repainting the Tower. In 1899 the company spent about £38,000 on the Matcham remodelling and the creation of the Tower Ballroom, as well as the café. The chairman noted at the 1899 shareholders' meeting that 'the almost universal opinion was that the Pavilion and Ballroom were the best, the finest and the handsomest they had ever seen or ever heard tell of.' He warned, though, that the Circus now suffered from comparison with the rest of the buildings and the directors were considering a scheme for redecoration of the Circus.

A shareholder, Mr Hutchinson, who had already quizzed the chairman on depreciation policy, asked how much the refurbishment would cost and whether it would be capitalised or expensed. 'I have not the slightest idea' replied Alderman Bickerstaffe (which is difficult to believe). Another shareholder suggested they left it to the directors. 'They know what they are doing. Where else can you find a company paying 6 per cent?' he observed (*Blackpool Gazette* 27 October 1899).

The work on the Circus took place over the close season and at the 1900 shareholders' meeting, held in the Circus, the chairman remarked that its appearance was now handsome and luxurious. He added that the increased expenditure had been quite justified by the additional receipts in connection with the Circus. One shareholder quipped that not only were the company's securities gilt-edged, so were its buildings.

The company also did some refinancing over this period. In addition to the new shares sold to finance the upgrade of the buildings, the company had replaced its £70,000 A Debenture which paid 5 per cent, with a new debenture paying 4½ per cent.

Bickerstaffe noted that the company's credit was now such that the whole issue had been taken up without having recourse to brokers and without paying any commission.

Another problem that rumbled on during this period was that the original share offer in 1891 had included a special category of shares known as 'founders' shares'. Only 5,000 of these were offered of which 4,785 were issued. These shareholders had, in addition to the normal dividend, a right to a further share of profits once the ordinary dividend reached 8 per cent. Holders of these shares started to ask questions at the shareholders' meetings, starting in 1898, as to when they were going to get more money. Bickerstaffe seems to have been reluctant to honour this special tranche of capital. At the time he pointed out that the ordinary dividend had not reached 8 per cent, so nothing was payable. He asked the holders of founders' shares to get together and put a proposition to the company.

In 1900 the company reported that it had sent a letter to the 220 people holding the shares, offering to exchange two founders' shares for three ordinary shares. While 132, representing 2,624 shares, had accepted, forty had refused and forty-eight had failed to reply, despite reminders. Insufficient votes had been received to enable the scheme to be carried out, but Bickerstaffe considered that the holders had been given the opportunity to participate in a 'fair, amicable and reasonable settlement'. It is not reported how this was resolved, but by 1909 the founders' shares had disappeared from the balance sheet.

The Alhambra Gamble

Not content with the refurbishment of the Tower buildings, in 1903 Bickerstaffe pulled off a coup by buying the Blackpool Alhambra Co. On paper the Alhambra Co. was bigger than the Tower Co., with total assets of £368,000, but it had gone bankrupt, and Bickerstaffe bought the company from the liquidator for a knock-down price of £137,000. Some people thought his ego had got the better of him – one of the Tower shareholders accused him publicly of thinking he was the uncrowned King of Blackpool and could do anything, but was actually about to bankrupt the Tower Co. Bickerstaffe countered that the Alhambra property adjoined that of the Tower, it was more valuable to the Tower Co. than anyone else, the Tower directors were clear why it had not made money in its past configuration, and were planning to spend about £25,000 to change it into a profitable venture.

Brian Turner and Steve Palmer[5] describe the genesis of the Alhambra. Like so many other local ventures, it was a standalone public company which in 1897 had easily raised £220,000 to buy land adjoining the Tower and construct the Alhambra, another entertainment centre incorporating a circus and a ballroom. The Alhambra opened on 22 May 1899, just as the Tower Co. unveiled its newly restyled Matcham ballroom. Turner and Palmer say the opening of the Alhambra was inauspicious as the walls had not yet been decorated and the building was unfinished. There was a second opening in July but the electrical equipment failed and the lifts remained unusable for the whole season.

They state that in 1900 the company began to run out of money and it made a loss of £47,000 in its first full season. 1901 was also loss-making and in 1902 creditors petitioned for the company to be liquidated. Turner and Palmer say (p61) the Alhambra was supposed to be the quintessential successful Blackpool entertainment centre.

It never really stood a chance, for not only was the site grossly-overvalued, but the building itself, beautiful though it was, was badly designed and inconveniently laid out. The poor shareholders had no hope of ever recovering any of their money.

The land on which the Alhambra had been built had been acquired for £224,000, at the height of a property boom in Blackpool,[6] and land values dropped dramatically shortly afterwards, which probably explained why Bickerstaffe was able buy the company at such a massive discount to the book value of its assets. The deal would have done nothing, however, to diminish Bickerstaffe's reputation as an aggressive deal-maker. The liquidator of the Alhambra held an auction at which Bickerstaffe bought much of its stocks in his own name, and the Alhambra Co. was sold to him personally. He then put the general manager of the Tower in charge and sold the whole thing to the Tower Co.

Many an entrepreneur would have taken a profit on the deal, but Bickerstaffe did not do so. He explained that it had not been legally possible for the Tower Co. to bid for the Alhambra, and therefore he had stepped in personally, but only on behalf of the Tower Co. It is very likely that the statutes of the Tower Co. had been drawn up on the basis of the company building and operating the Tower, and not providing for any other activity, or there were restrictions on its borrowing or equity.

This would have been easy enough to change, but would take time. Bickerstaffe therefore arranged personal borrowing, secured against the Alhambra, in order to complete the purchase. That he could do that says a lot about his personal standing and creditworthiness in Blackpool at that time, and also his risk-taking attitude – he would have had to sign up for the Alhambra and the debt without any legal certainty that the Tower Co. could or would take over the deal.

However, the whole deal was fully discussed with the Tower Co. board before anything was signed. They agreed that they needed to raise £160,000 to finance the acquisition and the remodelling. This would be done by issuing a further debenture for £100,000, and raising £60,000 from the issue of new shares.[7] The board members between them agreed to subscribe £10,000 of the new shares.

The company called an extraordinary shareholders meeting in July 1903 to seek approval for the financing and the purchase. Bickerstaffe told the shareholders, meeting in the Tower Pavilion on a Monday lunchtime, that the debenture had already been arranged, and that the share offer would be made in September, to give people time to make cash available if they wanted to buy more shares. The new shares would be sold at their £1 face value, thereby giving purchasers the incentive of a discount to the current market price. Although the share offer would be to the public at large, preference would be given to existing shareholders and debenture holders in allocating the new shares. There was no obligation to make a rights issue to existing shareholders at that time, which is the way such an issue would normally be handled now.

Bickerstaffe expressed his sympathy with the former shareholders of the Alhambra who had lost their money, but added that the company had to look at these matters in a calm, careful, practical and businesslike way. There was no disguising the fact that the Alhambra was built, that it was on the [sea] front, that it was in the market place, that it was in as good a position as the Tower and the Tower Co., and that it would have to be reckoned with. They had to consider whether it would be to the advantage or disadvantage of the Tower Co. if the Alhambra got into the hands of a powerful company with plenty of money behind it.

He said the directors were satisfied that by judicious alterations they could make the Alhambra profitable. But looking at it in the worst light, if it only succeeded in paying interest on the capital, it would still be of great benefit to the Tower Co. They could manage the Alhambra so that it did not compete or clash with the Tower entertainments.

He summed up that there were seven good reasons why the Tower Co. should purchase the Alhambra. First, the purchase price was little, it was virtually a break-up price; second, they would dispense with a competitor; third, there would be a great decrease in management expenses; fourth, there would be an increase in the revenue of the Tower Co.; fifth, nobody had yet made the Alhambra pay, but the Tower Co. could (applause);

sixth, the Alhambra was worth more to the Tower Co. than anyone else, and seventh, they had secured finance for two-thirds of the purchase price on very favourable terms and with no underwriting costs.

There was only one dissenting voice in the ballroom – Sidney Macfarlane, a shareholder from Burnley, opposed the motions in front of the meeting, saying that the Alhambra had never paid and would never pay. The reason the Alhambra debenture holders were willing to sell at such a price was because they believed nobody could make it pay. He said the Tower Co. was having difficulty paying a decent dividend already and there was no likelihood of the Alhambra paying. He proposed a motion that the Tower Co. should not buy the Alhambra, but no other shareholder present was willing to second the motion, let alone vote for it. Bickerstaffe, in a typical gesture, told the shareholders they could pick up tickets for the Alhambra at the end of the meeting and go to look around what they had just bought.

The Alhambra passed formally into the hands of the Tower Co. in November 1903. The share issue was massively oversubscribed, and work started on reconfiguring the building, once more under the supervision of Frank Matcham. It reopened on 4 July 1904, now called the Palace. Turner and Palmer[8] say that in the redesign the circus on the ground floor was closed, and the ballroom was moved down into its place. They say it became one of Blackpool's most popular entertainment centres for the next fifty years. The Tower Co. created what they called a 'panopticon' (a multi-purpose hall) in the space that had previously been the ballroom, and included film projection equipment in its facilities. The company subsequently incorporated a dedicated cinema into the property in 1911.

At the end of the 1904 season, Bickerstaffe reported to shareholders that pessimistic views of the Alhambra purchase had been refuted. It had not been a drag on the Tower Company's profits, and the dividend would be maintained (they had issued more Tower Co. shares to finance the purchase, and therefore more cash was needed if all shareholders were still to get the same percentage on their capital. This had been generated by the investment).

The Grand Theatre

In the nineteenth century theatre had been the poor relation of other forms of entertainment in Blackpool. Various venues had opened, only to close again after a short interval. This changed in the 1880s with the arrival of Thomas Sergenson in Blackpool. Initially he leased two theatres, the Prince of Wales and the Theatre Royal. In 1887 he bought property in Church Street which he proposed to knock down and replace with a theatre and five shops. Turner and Palmer[9] report that his plans were put into question when the Winter Gardens Co. decided to construct the Opera House (again the architect was Frank Matcham), which opened in 1889 with a production of *The Yeoman of the Guard* by the D'Oyly Carte Co. Sergenson built his shops but it was not until 1894 that he added the theatre, also designed by Matcham – which came to be known as 'Matcham's Masterpiece', now a Grade II-listed building.

The Blackpool Grand Theatre and Opera House Co. was registered in February 1894 with a capital of £20,000, made up of £100 shares. The Grand was a success. Sergenson brought some of the greats of British theatre to Blackpool, including Herbert Beerbohm Tree, Ellen Terry, Sarah Bernhardt and Lily Langtree. The manager had arrangements with some London theatres to host their productions.

He eventually sold the theatre in 1909 to the Tower Co. for £47,500, according to its history as published on its website. The Tower Co.'s financial statements showed new assets of freehold land £30,634 and buildings of £18,202, as well as plant of £2,693.[10] No information is given in the financial statements as to whether all of the new expenditure related to the Grand Theatre. The Tower Co. also took on a mortgage owed by the Grand Theatre of £16,480. Sergenson's motives for selling are not clear, but Bickerstaffe may have made him an offer he could not refuse. Barry Band says that in both 1908 and 1909 Sergenson had let the theatre for three months to a variety agent. He may have been having difficulty filling it all year round at that point.

Conclusion

In the twenty years between the completion of the Tower in 1894 and the outbreak of the First World War, John Bickerstaffe made it clear that he was prepared to make the Blackpool Tower Co. a major entertainments provider across Blackpool. He could have left the Tower Co. to operate its successful property, without expanding it, as was the case with the other major operators such as the Winter Gardens Co. and the Blackpool Pier Co. (North Pier). He could have expanded his own interests in activities outside the Tower Co. In fact he continued to invest personally in other projects, and was active in pursuing the provision of clean water to Blackpool, eventually becoming chairman of the Fylde Water Co. At the same time he expanded the Tower Co., first with the bold acquisition of the Alhambra, and subsequently with the acquisition of the Grand Theatre. Within the original property he continued to upgrade the premises, providing the now famous Matcham-designed Tower Ballroom.

He is described in the reports of shareholder meetings as 'a charmer' and as always jovial and friendly towards the shareholders. The *Blackpool Gazette* of 31 October 1911, for example, starts its report of the shareholders' meeting as follows: 'A particularly happy spirit prevailed at the twentieth annual meeting of the shareholders of the Blackpool Tower Co., held in the Tower Circus on Saturday afternoon, thanks, in no small measure, to the geniality of the chairman, Ald. John Bickerstaffe, JP, who was in characteristic good humour, as he sat behind the glass of 'something sparkling' – his customary companion – and … wore a buttonhole of Lilies of the Valley.'

In fact 1911 was a bad season for the company, and profits were down just after it had acquired the Grand Theatre. He explained that the season had been the 'finest and hottest, and had the least rainfall for thirty years'. He had never seen so many visitors before on the resort's 'golden sands'. Unfortunately they were not, as a consequence, spending their money at indoor places of entertainment. On top of that there had been a railway strike on the August bank holiday. At that particular meeting the shareholders nonetheless left happy, not least because the company had maintained the dividend despite the reduced profit. Bickerstaffe also succeeded in having his younger brother Tom Bickerstaffe elected to the board at this meeting to replace one of the founding directors who had died.

He was innovative in terms of shareholder relations, with gestures such as providing tickets for the shareholders to inspect the Alhambra, and having a lion on hand to entertain. Later meetings refer to his technique of starting the meeting at noon, to be followed by drinks and a buffet on the company's premises, so shareholders would not want to linger too long on questions to the board.

6

THE FIRST WORLD WAR

The First World War was a difficult time for the Tower Co. On the financial front, the government introduced a number of new taxes – especially the Entertainment Tax – and increased normal income tax, so the state started taking a much bigger share of the profits than it had done previously. As far as holidaymakers were concerned, the railways were put under government control and there were at first no more daytrips or other excursions to Blackpool to bring in visitors. There was also a shortage of men and materials so it was impossible to carry out routine maintenance, let alone improvements. On the positive side, troops were billeted in Blackpool because of its facilities to provide not only accommodation but also large indoor spaces in which training could be carried out. While the influx of summer visitors was reduced, there were visitors all year round, and shows which would normally have been staged in London were put on in Blackpool.

The table below shows the reported[1] profit before interest and depreciation[2] over this period:

Season	Operating Profit £
1910	38,670
1911	33,061
1912	40,567
1913	44,670
1914	27,678
1915	28,365

Season	Operating Profit
1916	33,299
1917	39,313
1918	51,463
1919	59,709
1920	70,103
1921	37,191
1922	24,343
1923	59,599

There was a dip in 1911 (caused by the unusually good weather which motivated people to sit on the beach instead of visiting the Tower), and then in 1914 business fell away. It began to revive in 1916 and reached pre-war levels in 1917, with a surge at the end of the war. Business fell off again in 1921 and 1922 which was a period marked by job insecurity, labour disputes and social unrest.

At the 1914 shareholders' meeting, the chairman reported that up to the end of July 1914 receipts had been ahead of the previous year, but when war was declared at the beginning of August 'the receipts went "wallop"'. The railways had been commandeered by the government and the railway companies had advised holidaymakers to get home as quickly as possible. Business picked up a little in September and October however (*Blackpool Gazette and News* 1 December 1914).

In 1916 John Bickerstaffe was absent from the annual meeting because he was in hospital having an operation. Robert Parker, the company secretary, reported increased profits. He said the directors considered this satisfactory in the circumstances. There had been an absence of cheap bookings, which had affected admissions, but there had been many soldiers billeted in the town and many new visitors, although the bars had suffered because of restrictions on opening hours. (*Blackpool Gazette and News* 5 December 1916).

The war had ended by the time of the 1918 shareholders' meeting and, prefacing his remarks by comments on the 'victory', chairman Bickerstaffe went on to remark that 'the West coast was the only safe place to which anyone could come and reside and enjoy themselves, where anything in the shape of entertainments had been going on.' (*Blackpool Gazette and News* 10 December 1918).

War Taxation

In the early days of the First World War, the government did not expect that the war would be very long, nor very expensive. They were wrong, and subsequently set out on a path of increasing tax rates and introducing new taxes to pay for the war effort. The most costly of these for the Tower Co. was Entertainments Tax, an excise duty which imposed a levy on admissions to places of entertainment. However the company was also affected by increases in excise duty on alcohol, as well as Excess Profits Duty and increases in income tax.

Rutterford and Walton[3] discuss the impact of wartime taxes on the company. They quote the January 1918 ERA Almanack, which gives the 1917 rates of Entertainments Tax:

Net price not exceeding	Tax
2d	½d
4d	1d
6d	2d
1s	3d
2s	4d
3s	6d
5s	9d

Like contemporary Value Added Tax, the tax was collected in the price to the final consumer, and the retailer was left with the choice of putting up prices, or absorbing the tax. For the Tower Co., the 6d admission to the complex had to go up to 8d, to collect 2d per person for the government. The impact was significant. At the 1916 shareholders' meeting, the company secretary revealed that the company had paid £9,422 after the imposition of the tax from 15 May 1916. 'It was paid by the people, collected at great trouble by the company and paid to the government, and the chairman hoped that when the war was over the impost would be discontinued.' (*Blackpool Gazette and News* 5 December 1916).

In fact Entertainments Tax remained in force until 1960. The impact on the company is given in Table 2. In 1919 the company contributed more than £50,000 in this tax:

	Tax paid £	Net Sales after ET (including bars, catering etc.) £	Tax as per cent of Sales before ET per cent
1916	9,422	165,698	5.38
1917	14,758	184,353	7.41
1918	36,899	263,795	12.27
1919	51,633	366,599	12.35
1920	53,833	418,290	11.40
1921	44,651	368,601	10.80
1922	43,292	338,741	11.33
1923	47,346	357,494	11.69
1924 (rate reduced)	40,383	365,182	9.96
1925	41,575	415,978	9.09
1926	41,861	413,166	9.20
1927	47,067	464,333	9.20
1928	46,319	453,908	9.26
1929	46,634	432,417	9.73
1930	41,383	405,378	9.26

Undoubtedly the imposition of the tax had the effect of reducing the company's profits. To some extent the impact was, however, reduced by inflation. The First World War was a period of significant inflation, and the company was able to increase prices as holidaymakers' wages increased. A variable admission to the complex was introduced, changing according to season and time of day. The top admission went up to 1s, of which 3d was tax, leaving the company with revenue of 9d – an increase of 50 per cent on pre-war figures, but asking the customer to pay twice as much as in 1914. The Tower Co. appears to have been able to absorb the change, but the cinema industry complained vociferously.

In 1922 cinema proprietors formed the Cinema Tax Abolition Committee which produced a campaigning pamphlet entitled 'The Crushing Entertainments Tax'. This offers the view that 'no trade can prosper under a burden of 25 per cent tax on its gross receipts over and above all other forms of taxation.' They argued that the tax was preventing proprietors from carrying out repairs to their buildings and reported that there was a drift downwards to the cheaper seats by customers.[4]

At the 1918 shareholders' meeting of the Tower Co., a shareholder (Mr Clough of Poulton, near Blackpool) queried that there was no mention of Entertainments Tax in the annual financial statements. Chairman Bickerstaffe replied that the amount paid was large and he did not think it should be made public. It is difficult to know why he was so coy about the numbers, especially since the company did publish them elsewhere. However, for a very long time companies regarded their total sales (or 'turnover') as highly confidential. Publication only became compulsory in the UK in 1982 when Britain enacted European rules on the subject. Bickerstaffe may have just been reflecting the general view on the confidentiality of corporate data, or more specifically that telling people how much Entertainments Tax the company paid would have given them a benchmark to estimate the sensitive turnover number.

Excess Profits Duty

For many, possibly most, companies, however, the most important tax in the First World War was Excess Profits Duty. This applied from 1914 and was addressed directly to companies that made increased profits as a result of the war. Some industries, especially food, shipping and obviously companies that produced munitions and other matériel, made vastly increased profits as a result of rapid price increases due to war shortages. Equally there was rapid inflation as well, which meant that even if a company was not directly affected by the war, it would be putting up its prices (albeit paying its staff more) as a result of inflation and so would be reporting increased paper profits, even if it is less clear that they were always making increased real profits, as the value of the pound decreased. This caused a considerable political outcry as the papers and politicians called for war profiteering to be addressed.

Excess Profits Duty was the government's response. In retrospect it was a clever tax which took seven years of activity, from 1914 to 1921, and taxed heavily all profits that were greater than the average profits in the three years before the war.[5] However, although the government stated when it introduced the tax that it was for the duration of the war, in principle UK taxes are enacted on a year to year basis, so many of the details of the administration of the tax emerged over time, and the closing date was not known until after the war.

It was as a consequence difficult for companies to know how much to estimate in the accounts for the tax charge year by year. In current corporate taxation, losses can be carried forward and offset against profits in future years, but with Excess Profits Duty the final charge was based on an average of seven years, so the definitive amount due could not be known until after 1921. Indeed, extending the tax to 1921 turned out to be a mistake for the government, because the economy turned down in that last year, which had the effect of reducing the overall bill for companies.

The same shareholder, Mr Clough of Poulton, asked the chairman at the 1918 shareholders' meeting how much Excess Profits Duty the company had paid. This was potentially a very sensitive question, because, if a company was paying Excess Profits Tax, it was, almost by definition, making excess profits and therefore a war profiteer, so companies were loath to admit to paying it. By 1918 the Tower Co. was indeed doing well out of the war. However, Bickerstaffe replied that it had to date paid none, although only the future could say whether they would eventually pay any.

Rutterford and Walton did an analysis of the Tower Co.'s Excess Profits Tax which suggests that Bickerstaffe was literally correct in his 1918 comment, but eventually slightly misleading. Because Excess Profits Duty was calculated on averages, years when a company made less than its pre-war average would reduce taxes in years when it made more. This was the case of the Blackpool Tower Co. From 1914 to 1917 it was making annual profits less than its 1912/13 average, and so it was accumulating a cushion, and the company probably did not have to part with any actual cash until 1919 and 1920, even though in 1918 it reported profits well above the pre-war average. This supports Bickerstaffe's comment at the 1918 meeting. However analysis suggests that the company probably set aside £10,000 in 1918 against a possible Excess Profits Duty charge for that year, even though by the time of the shareholders' meeting this would certainly not have led to any physical payment to the government because of the cumulative effect and the time taken to agree tax returns.

Profits and Reported Profits

Financial reporting today is much different to what it was at the beginning of the twentieth century. There was then no obligation to provide a detailed profit and loss account (detail of the year's trading) and there were none of the pages of explanatory notes to be found in a modern financial report. Some people think that part of the reason for the change is that a hundred years ago most listed companies were small, local concerns. The shareholder could easily get to the annual meeting, visit the company's locations and generally see what was going on. There were no complicated finance issues, no foreign currency nor overseas operations. Most of the Tower shareholders were from the north-west, meetings were held in the Tower Circus or Pavilion, and all the company's activities were within a short distance from there. The chairman usually gave a detailed verbal commentary on the accounts and the activities of the year just passed at the annual meeting.

The company did not publish a detailed profit or loss account, nor did it separate out taxation in the published statements. The Tower Co. 1910 accounts, which were typical, gave the following data:

	£
Net revenue from Tower, Palace and Grand Theatre	38,671
Interest received on investment	355
Total	39,026
Less	
Interest on Grand Theatre Mortgage	(586)
Interest on debentures	(9400)
Bank interest	(208)
Total finance cost	(10,194)
Sub-total	28,832
Other deductions	
Depreciation	(8,500)
Reserve fund	(1,032)
Maintenance fund	(3,000)
Capital expenses	(597)
Net	15,703
Dividend paid	(14,560)

The information was not displayed in exactly this form, it has been reformulated to make clear the message the directors were sending: the profit for the year was £15,703 and the dividend paid was £14,560. This is what the shareholders expected to see. They considered that buying company shares was almost like putting money in the bank – you expected the company would pay out its full profits and provide an annual return of maybe 5 per cent or more.[6]

The trouble with this was that it drained the company of excess cash, so it had no 'war chest' it could call on to invest in its assets or to absorb losses in bad years. Company management therefore used devices like depreciation, maintenance funds and 'reserves' to reduce the apparent profit. You can see here that the profit was £28,832 after paying interest charges but before other charges. The other charges are more or less at the management's discretion and do not involve any cash leaving the company, so enabling it to conserve nearly half of the year's profit within the company.

Depreciation is the most debatable of these charges. Current practice would say that assets are being consumed and this should be reflected in the company's annual profit, but there was no requirement then, and indeed the Tower Co. did not charge any depreciation at all in 1921 and for several years afterwards. At the time there was a view that by repairing the assets as necessary you preserved their working life, and the appropriate treatment was to charge repairs against the year's profits but not to depreciate the underlying asset – a view held by some hotel companies today. These discretionary charges were used to manipulate the profit available for shareholders, as the following table shows:

	Deductions from profit		
Year	Maintenance	Reserves	Depreciation
	£	£	£
1914	-	-	8,500
1915	-	-	8,500
1916	3,000	-	8,500
1917	5,000	2,500	8,500
1918	10,000	5,000	8,500
1919	10,000	10,000	8,500
1920	-	37,500	8,500
1921	10,000	-	-

Source: Blackpool Tower Co. Ltd annual statements

The pattern of voluntary deductions matched that of the change in profits. Of course, managing shareholder perceptions was not the only issue. The company was aware that the Tower was badly in need of maintenance by the end of the war, as neither men nor materials had been available to maintain it normally during the war period. The company did have a genuine need to address a growing maintenance problem, but it did also subsequently use its reserves to make a bonus issue of shares.[7] This kind of reasonably transparent manipulation of the profit available for shareholders was the norm at the time, and is one reason why year on year comparisons can be difficult. The lack of disclosure of taxation is also a problem because the company, like all others at the time, went through a period of considerable increase in taxation and some volatility, none of which was visible in the published financial statements.

Maintenance

In fact the whole of the Tower Co. properties had to be renovated after the war. The normal seasonal cycle had been disturbed by the war – instead of everything being closed in the winter, and that time used for maintenance, many businesses had remained open all year round, given the continuing presence of troops and others in the town. On top of that there had been a shortage of both materials and manpower because of the war. In 1919 the Tower Co. reverted to the normal seasonal cycle. At the 1920 shareholders' meeting, John Bickerstaffe announced that redecorations and repairs had been done to the Tower, the Palace, the Tower Circus and the Palace Theatre. He said the company's properties 'had been put in excellent condition' and added that they were starting work on the Tower structure and the Grand Theatre.

He commented that many enquiries had been received as to the state of the Tower. It had been inspected by the contractors who had originally built it, and one of the chief engineers. 'When the extensive overhauling, scraping and repainting had been done, it would again be as strong as ever.' (*Blackpool Gazette and News* 21 December 1920).

The following year he told shareholders that 'they were spending a very considerable amount of money on the Tower in renewals and painting' (no figure is given). They had been advised by the engineers that by doing this during the next few years they could give the Tower another fifteen or twenty years' life. 'I do not know what your opinion is,' the chairman said, 'I can tell you that the opinion of this board is that Blackpool would not be Blackpool without the Tower.' (*Blackpool Gazette and News* 13 December 1921).

At the 1922 meeting he gave more detail, saying that the cost of making good the effects of corrosion had been exacerbated by the fact that, as a result of the war, they had not been able to do annual maintenance. He said that trying to overtake the corrosion some two or three years afterwards was a very extensive process and cost a considerable amount more in the replacement of material than if it had been dealt with year by year. He said the additional expense had been charged against the profits since 1920, and the work was expected to be complete by the end of the 1923 season. (*Blackpool Gazette and News* 5 December 1922)

However, work was not limited to the Tower. The accounts for 1921 show £13,797 spent on the Grand Theatre, a considerable sum for the time. The shareholders meeting revealed that extensive work was also being carried out at the Palace Picture Theatre. Bickerstaffe remarked that although pictures had been shown there successfully in the past, they could not call it an ideal picture theatre. Now it was due for redecoration, repainting and they found that by spending an extra £10,000 they would have an up-to-date theatre with a considerable increase in seating accommodation. It would be 'the prettiest and most attractive picture house in the whole country'.

The following year he announced a total expenditure of £25,251, saying it was now a very handsome building and would likely please the most fastidious of tastes. The work on the Palace had caused a reduction in takings, as it was normally open during the winter. The film shows had been transferred to the Tower Ballroom, but that had involved a loss of takings and extra cost, as well as the ballroom not making a very satisfactory cinema. However, he announced that the whole range of the company's buildings were now in a thoroughly up-to-date condition and the directors did not anticipate any further expenditure upon those buildings for many years to come. (*Blackpool Gazette and News* 5 December 1922).

Conclusion

It might be said that the company 'had a good war' – or at least that it came out of the war better than it might have done, even if it had a significant amount of expenditure after the war to make good the wear and tear, and to get the premises into a pristine state. It was a hallmark of Bickerstaffe's success that he always believed that money spent making the buildings of the highest quality came back in holidaymaker spending.

The company survived the Entertainments Tax which brought severe difficulties for many other entertainment companies at that time, and avoided paying a significant amount of Excess Profits Duty. Its profitability did, however, become something of a roller-coaster ride. A bad downturn in 1914 and 1915 turned into big profits in 1917, 1918 and 1919 but then fell off again. Dividends were cut, then nearly doubled, then cut again. Despite this, Bickerstaffe seems always to have had a good reception from his shareholders who understood the context in which the company was operating.

There was only one slight interruption to the unsullied love affair between the chairman and his shareholders. Mr Clough (from Poulton) objected at the 1919 meeting to the directors being paid their salaries (£400 for Bickerstaffe, £300 each for the others) free of taxes. He said that this had been exceptional and should not be automatic. The chairman was annoyed and implied that he would resign if Mr Poulton's motion was approved. Of course it was rejected, but the following year, when Bickerstaffe held an extraordinary meeting to change the company's articles in order to allow it to increase the share capital, he also introduced a new article requiring directors' salaries to be free of tax. Income tax was not that high at the time, but had been increased significantly during the First World War and would continue to increase in the future.

7

THE WINTER GARDENS CO.

The 1920s were John Bickerstaffe's fourth and last decade at the helm of the Blackpool Tower Co. This decade was marked by his knighthood in 1926 and above all by the acquisition in 1928 of the Tower Company's biggest local rival, the Winter Gardens Co. When Sir John died on 5 August 1930, he could indeed have felt he had earned the title King of Blackpool: born on the sea front, he had constructed the icon with which the resort still remains most identified, he had played a major part in the construction of civic Blackpool, and he had run its most successful company.

The decade was not the easiest financially for the company. It had come out of the First World War reasonably successfully, having absorbed major tax increases and making more profit. However 1920 was the zenith and profits tailed off quickly in 1921 and 1922, turning round in 1923 but only getting back to the 1920 high-water mark in 1925. In 1921 the chairman cited the coal strike and other industrial unrest as the cause of the downturn, and in 1922 he noted that visitor numbers were up but people seemed to have less money to spend. He quoted the prime minister as reassuring people that trade would recover in 1923, which up to a point it did.

However, the fall-off in receipts gave the company a number of financial problems. The various buildings belonging to the company had not been maintained during the war, and the company had embarked on what turned out to be a five-year programme of extensive renovations, all of which were charged against profits. At the same time, the board seemed quite optimistic about the future and set out on a series of property acquisitions. It is a classic in the life of a company that after being a lean and aggressive challenger, if it succeeds, it starts to build up its own internal infrastructure. This has been referred to as 'overhead creep' and occurs because as companies grow they need a more elaborate management structure, and as they make profits they feel they ought to do things 'properly'. As a consequence they have more extensive costs. If they do not continue to grow, then sooner or later these need to be trimmed to restore profitability.

In the case of the Tower Co., its overheads grew through the acquisition of offices next to the Grand Theatre, and through various properties around Blackpool which the management felt were needed for storage, workshops and stables. The company also acquired new commercial property in the form of a series of purchases which gave it a 350-foot frontage on Central Beach. This was an area just to the south of the Tower and known to John Bickerstaffe since his father's Wellington Hotel was there and also the South Jetty pier – now renamed the Central Pier.

The block acquired by the Tower Co. included a restaurant. When asked what the company planned to do with it, the chairman initially said he was not at liberty to explain, but that they would run the café/restaurant themselves. He said it was a strategic purchase – and indeed history would prove him right because sea-front property would become increasingly difficult to find and expensive to buy.

However, another possible explanation is that the company did not in fact have the cash to develop the Central Beach property at that juncture. It had entered into purchase contracts with settlement due several months after the deals had been done.

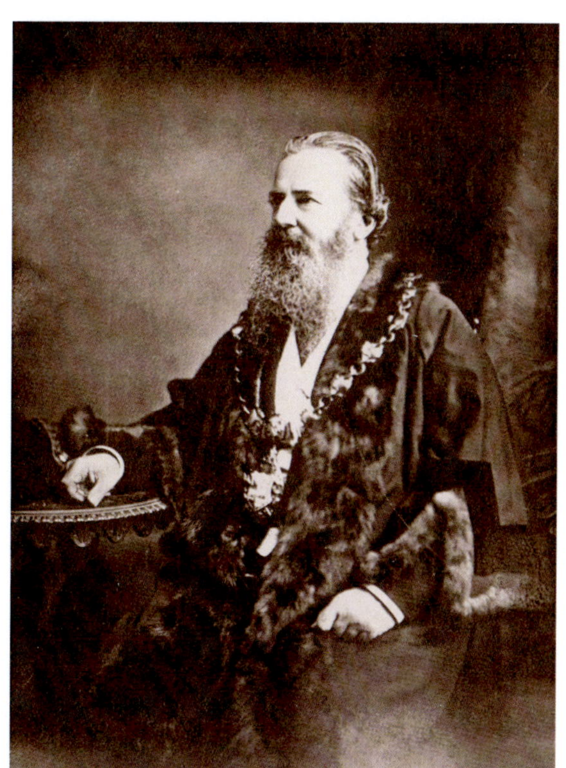

Dr W. H. Cocker – first mayor of
Blackpool.

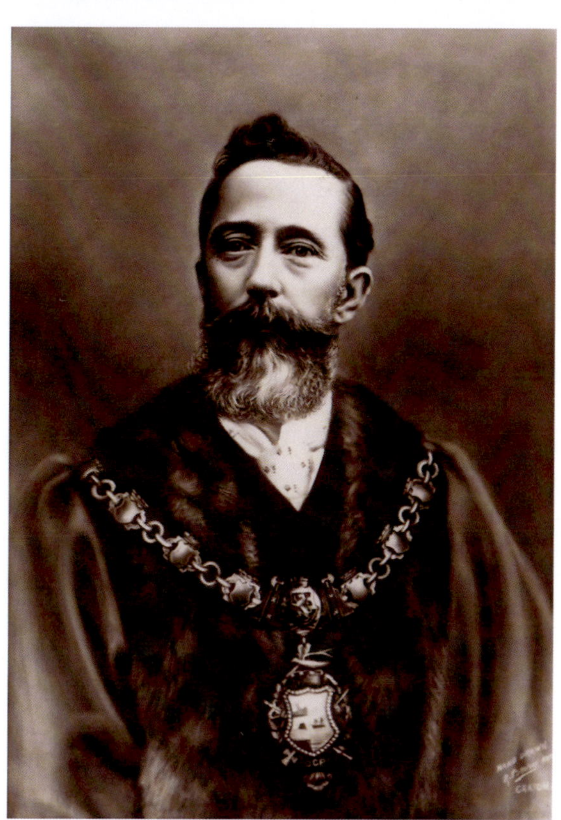

Mayor John Bickerstaffe, *c.* 1890.

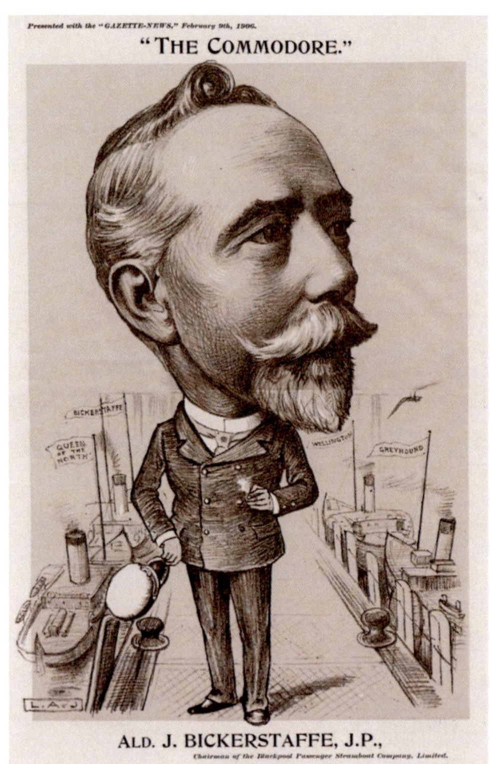

ALD. J. BICKERSTAFFE, J.P.,
Chairman of the Blackpool Passenger Steamboat Company, Limited.

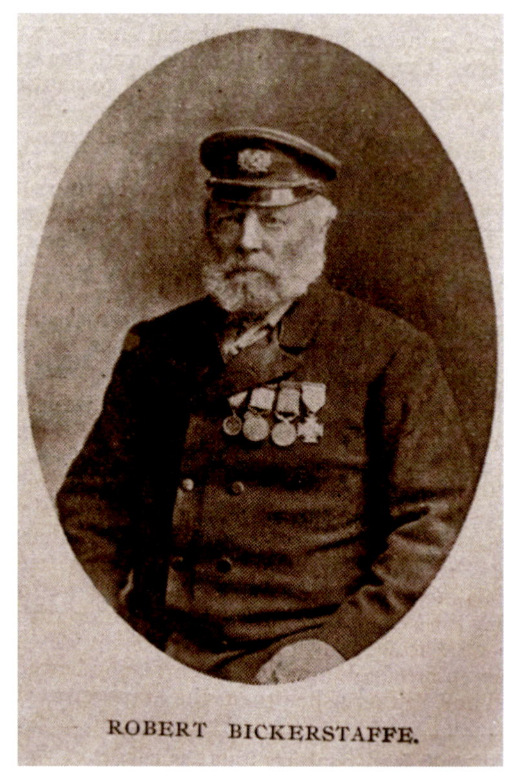

ROBERT BICKERSTAFFE.

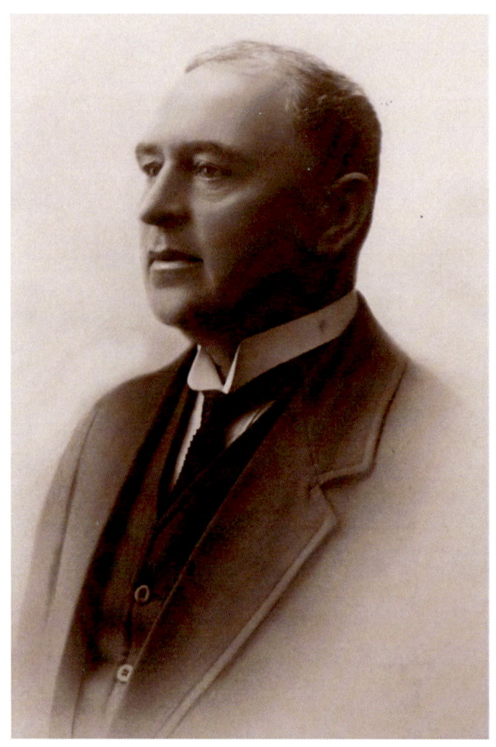

Top left: Cartoon of John Bickerstaffe.

Top right: Robert Bickerstaffe Senior.

Left: Thomas Bickerstaffe.

Right: Advert for South Jetty Co., 1890.

Bottom left: Architect's drawing of Douglas Tower.

Bottom right: Architect's drawing of Blackpool Tower.

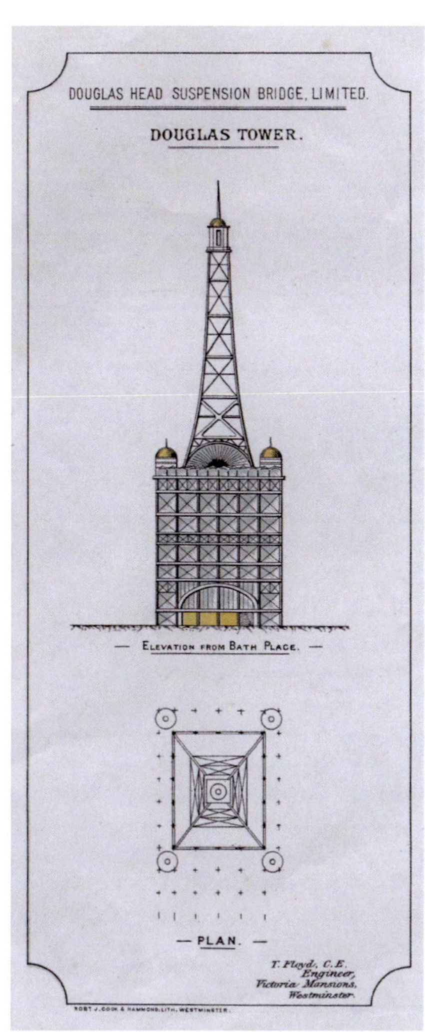

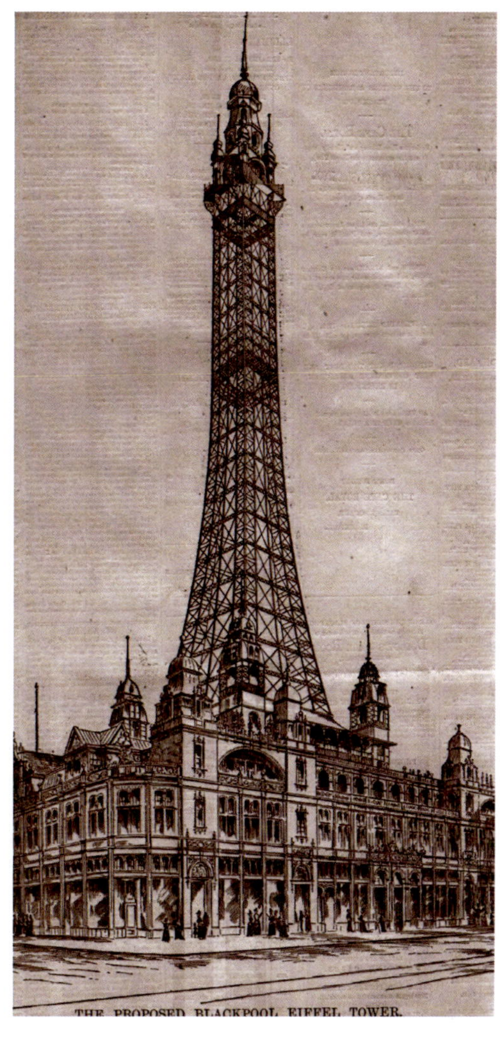

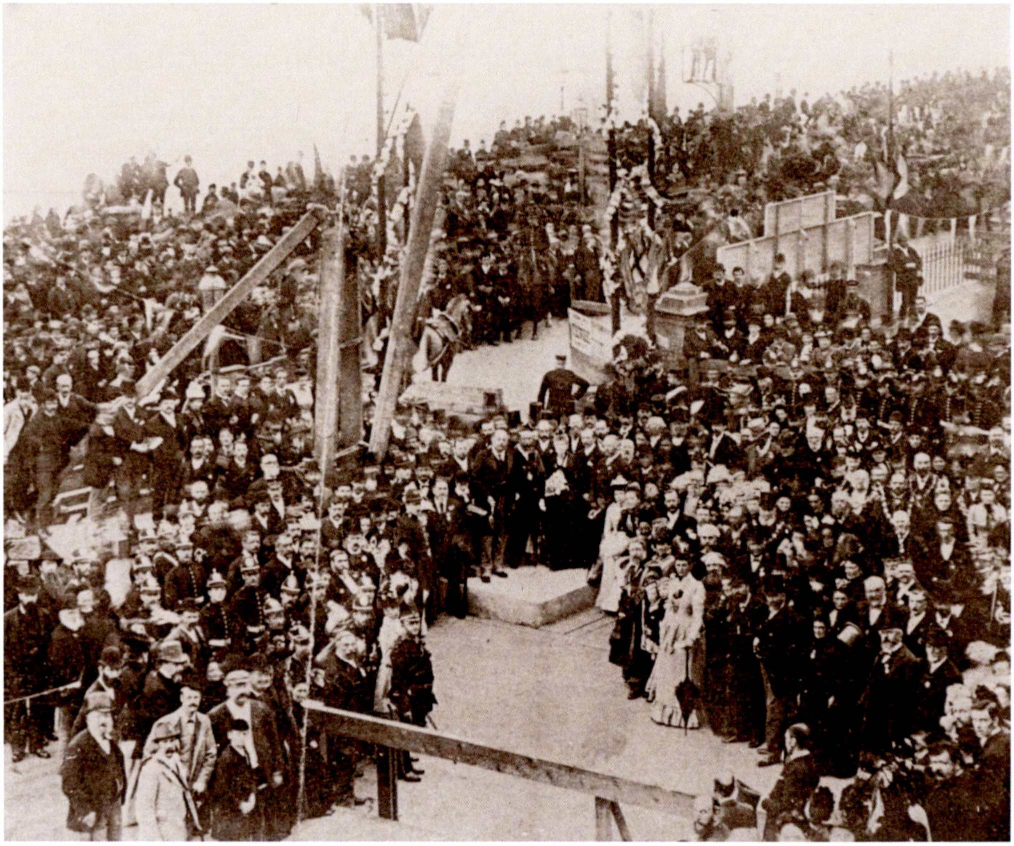

Top: Laying foundation stone, 25 September 1891.

Bottom: Aquarium entrance before construction, 1892.

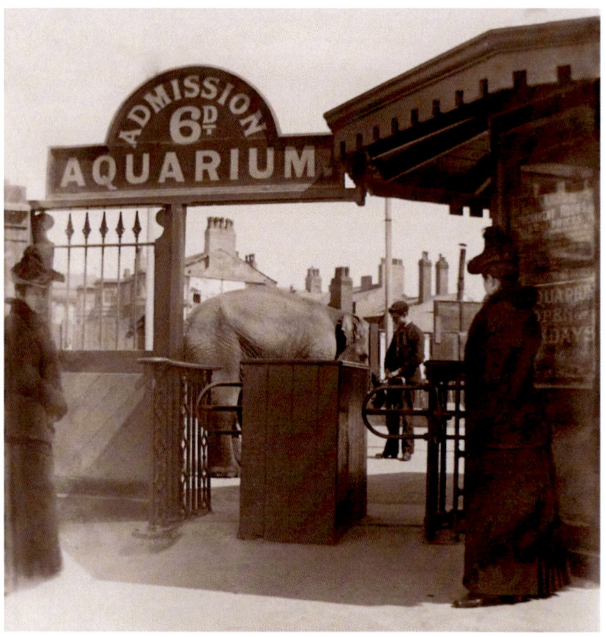

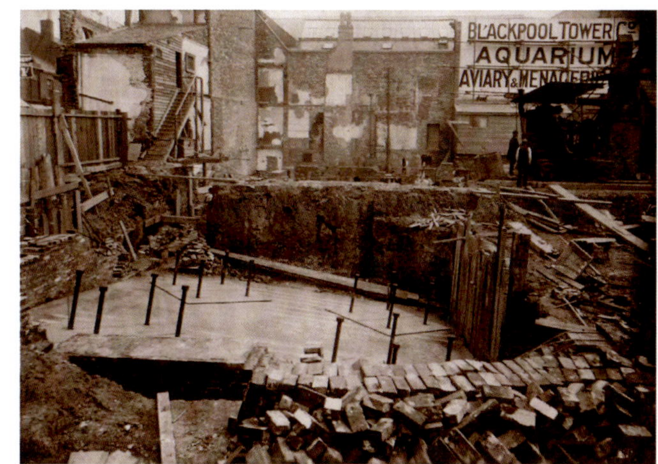

Tower foundations being dug.

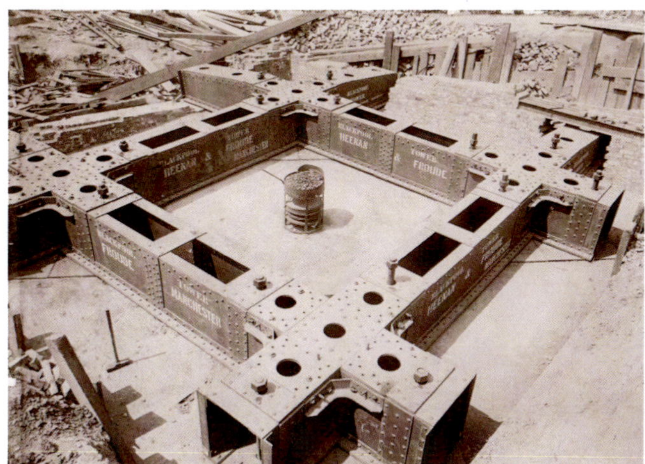

Tower foundations.

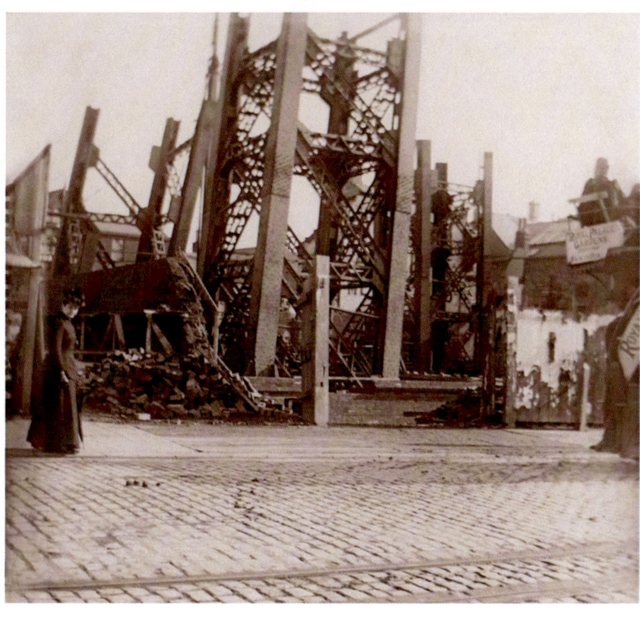

Tower construction, 1892.

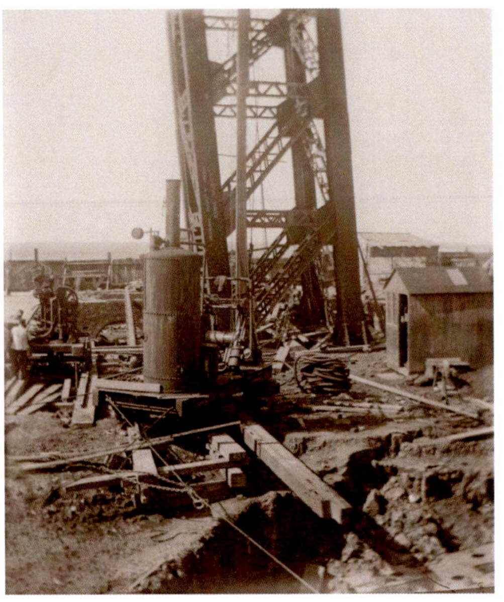

One of the main legs, 1892.

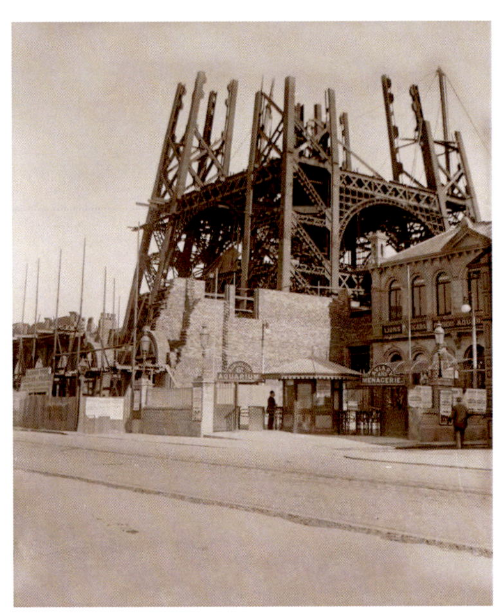

Tower constructed round Aquarium, 1893.

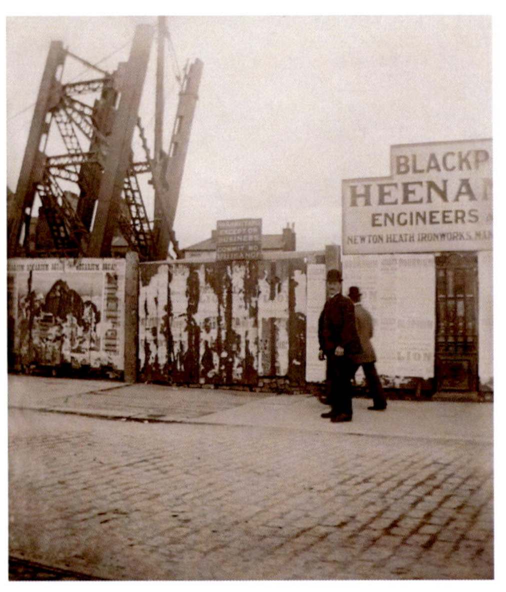

Site showing Heenan's hoarding.

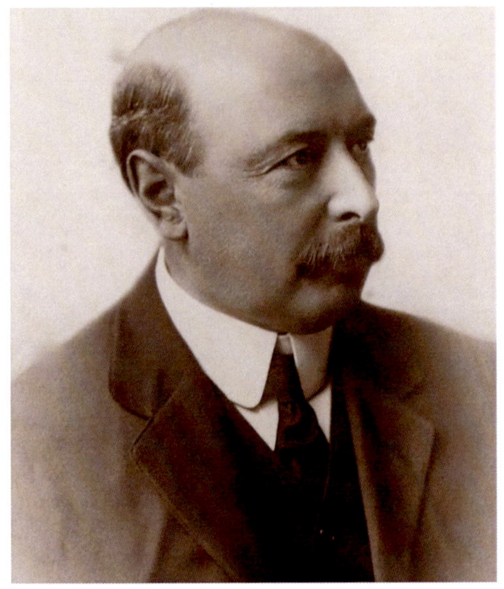

Thomas Smethurst, the auditor.

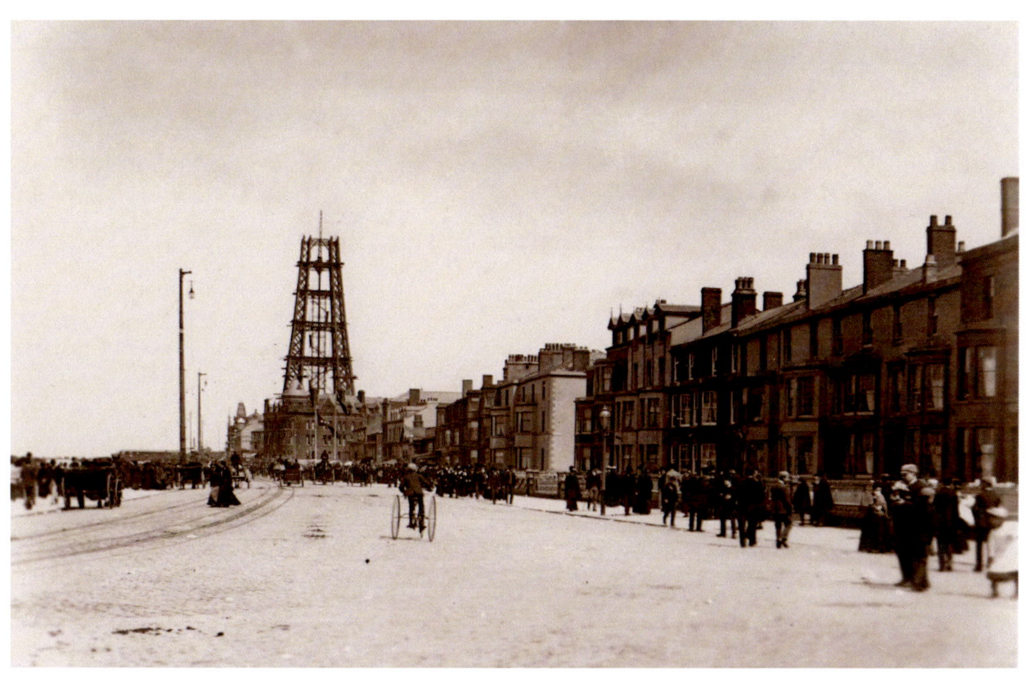

Top: Tower growing in 1893.

Right: Tower opened in 1894, some buildings not complete.

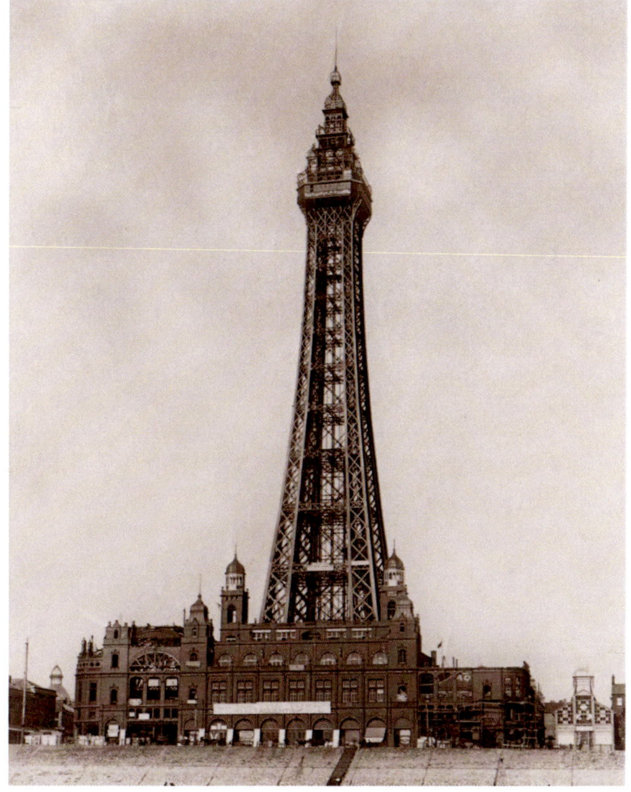

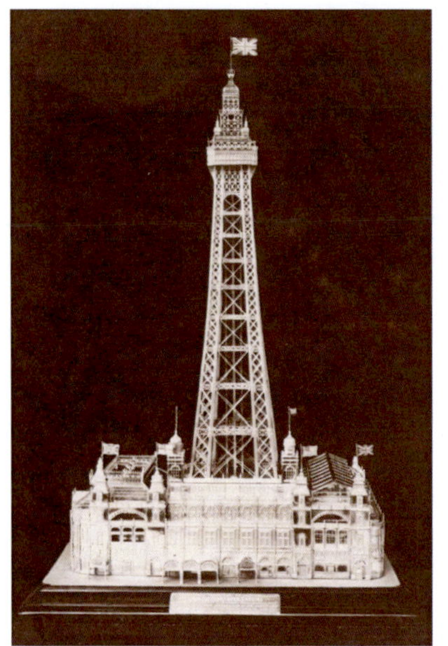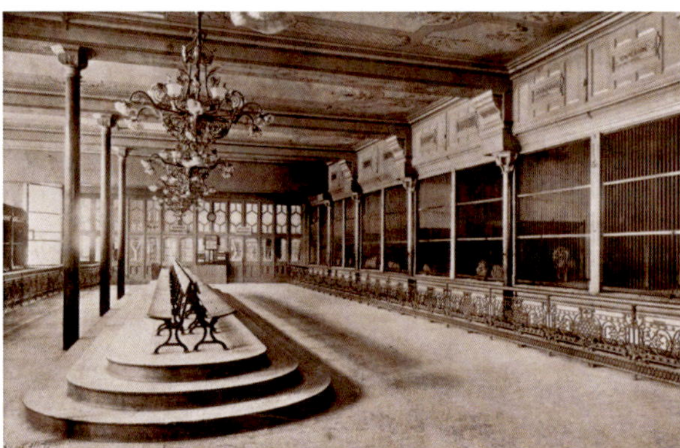

Top left: Silver replica presented by shareholders to chairman.

Top right: Tower menagerie, *c*. 1900.

Bottom: Tower Roof Gardens, *c*. 1900.

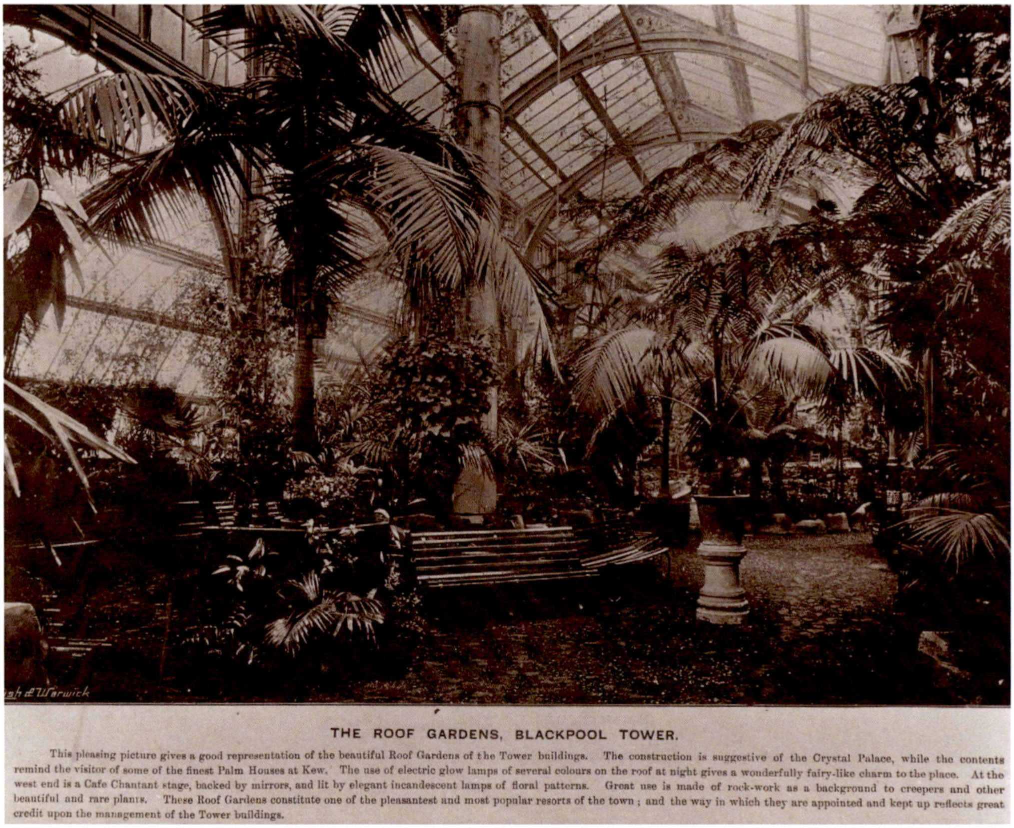

THE ROOF GARDENS, BLACKPOOL TOWER.

This pleasing picture gives a good representation of the beautiful Roof Gardens of the Tower buildings. The construction is suggestive of the Crystal Palace, while the contents remind the visitor of some of the finest Palm Houses at Kew. The use of electric glow lamps of several colours on the roof at night gives a wonderfully fairy-like charm to the place. At the west end is a Cafe Chantant stage, backed by mirrors, and lit by elegant incandescent lamps of floral patterns. Great use is made of rock-work as a background to creepers and other beautiful and rare plants. These Roof Gardens constitute one of the pleasantest and most popular resorts of the town; and the way in which they are appointed and kept up reflects great credit upon the management of the Tower buildings.

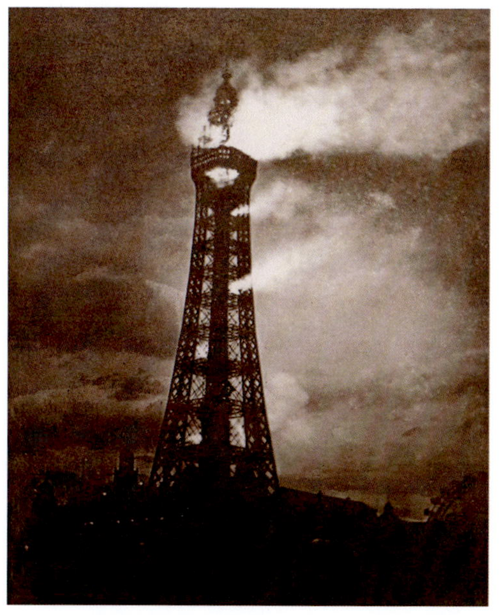

Tower fire, 1897.

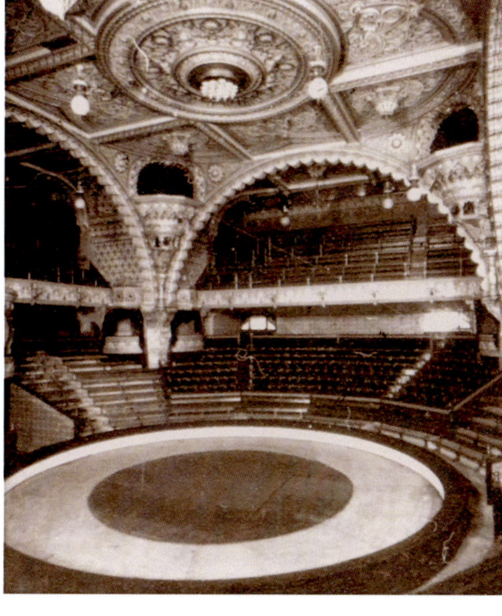

Tower Circus.

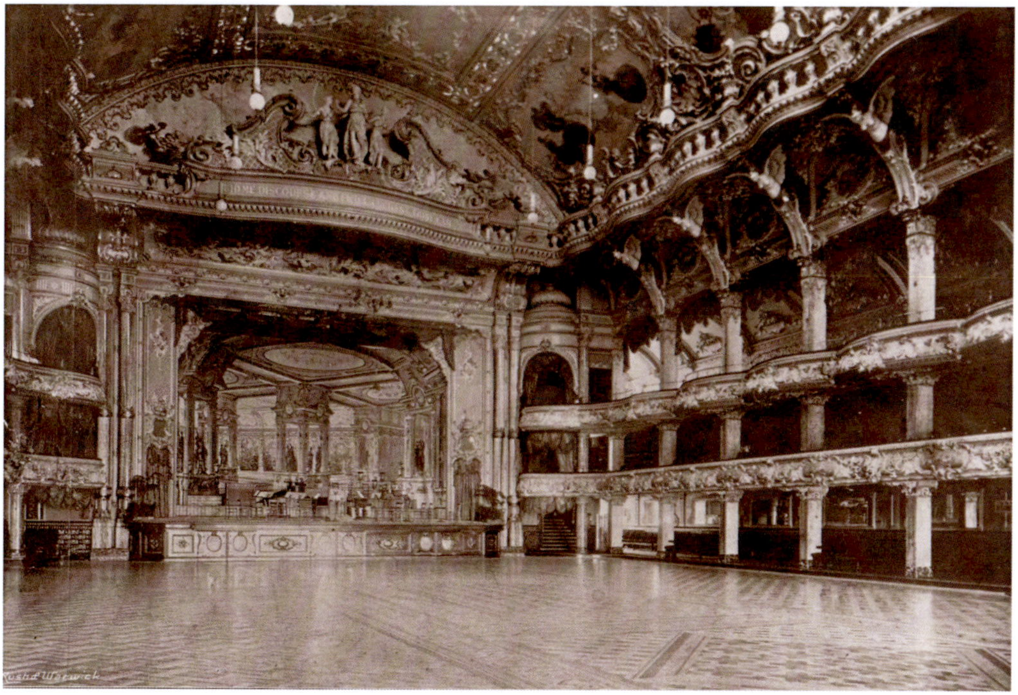

Tower Ballroom after Matcham refurbishment.

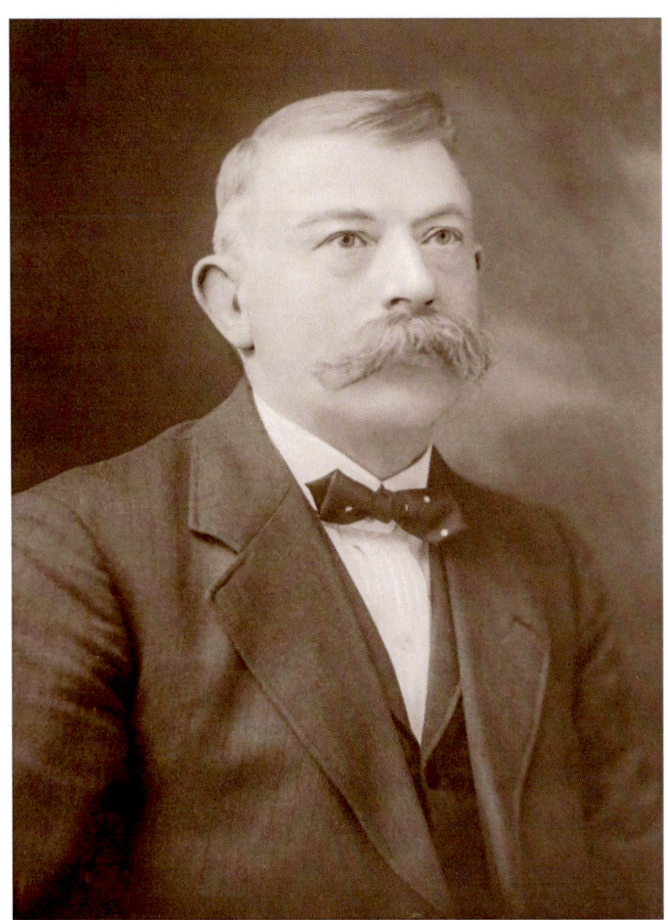

Left: George Harrop, general manager.

Bottom: The Alhambra is now the Palace.

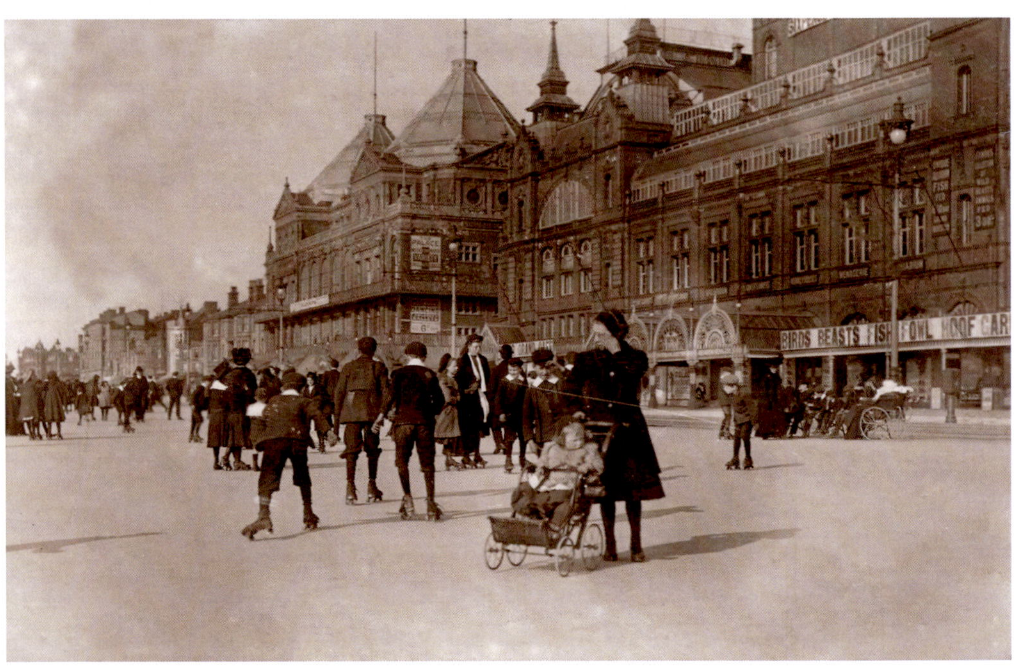

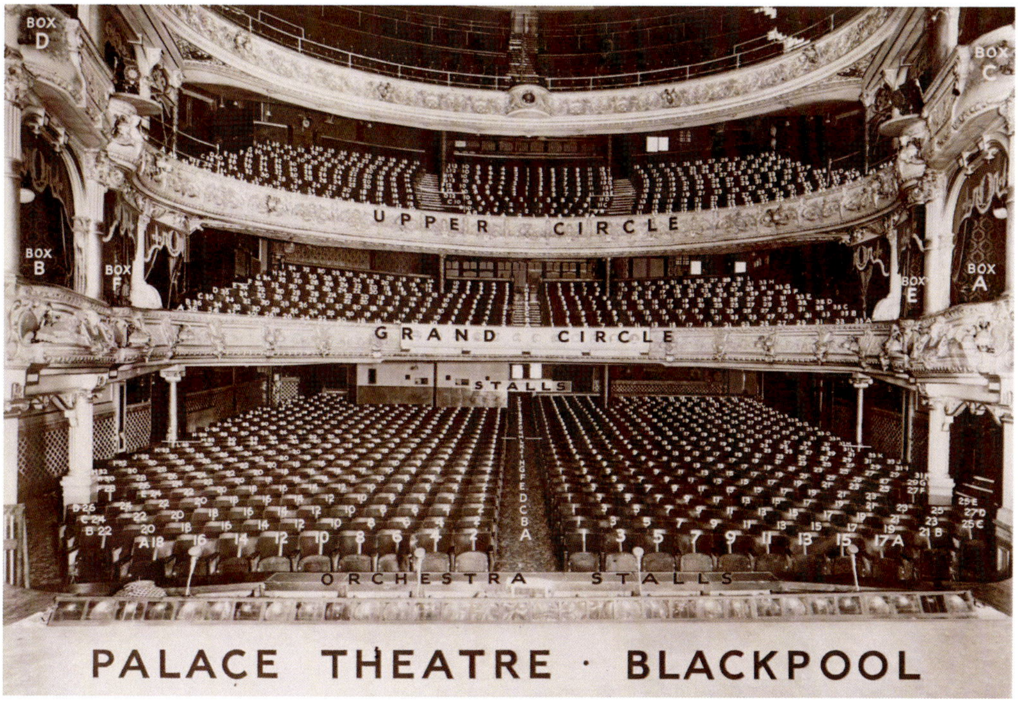

Top: Interior of Palace Theatre.

Bottom left: Grand Theatre.

Bottom right: Interior of Grand Theatre.

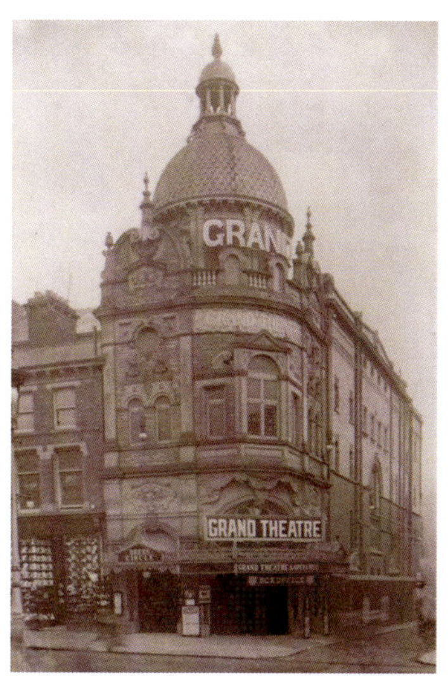
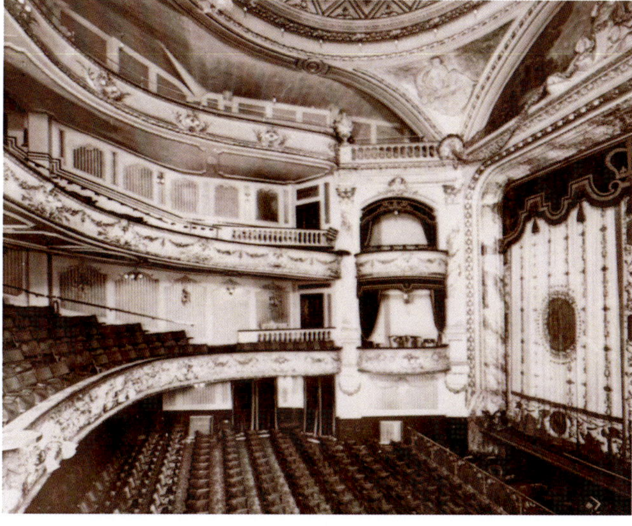

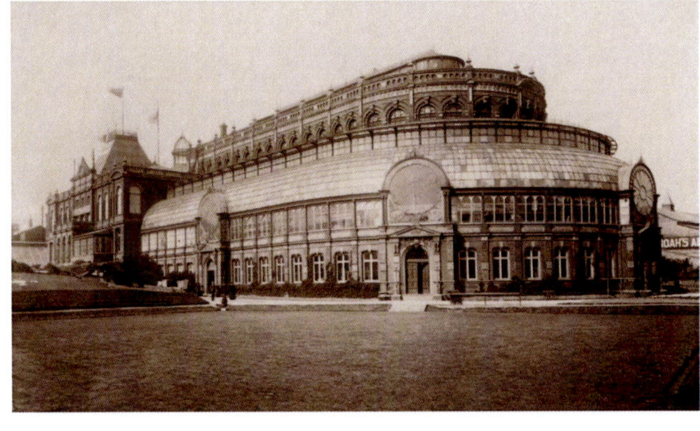

Winter Gardens *c.* 1893.

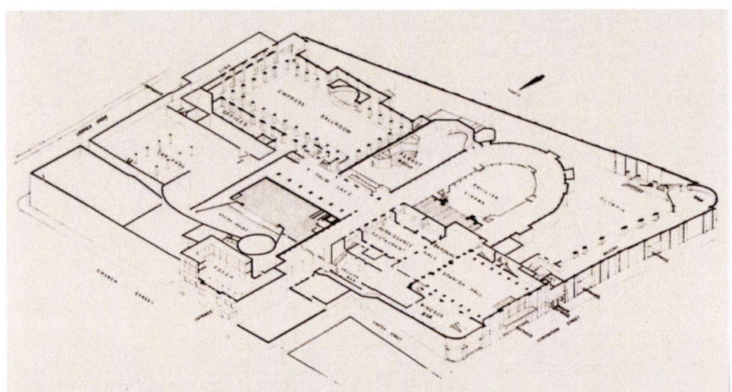

Winter Gardens after adding the Opera House and the Empress Ballroom.

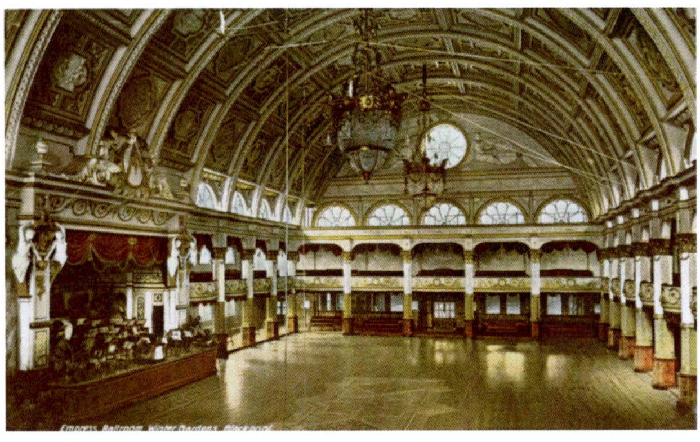

Empress Ballroom.

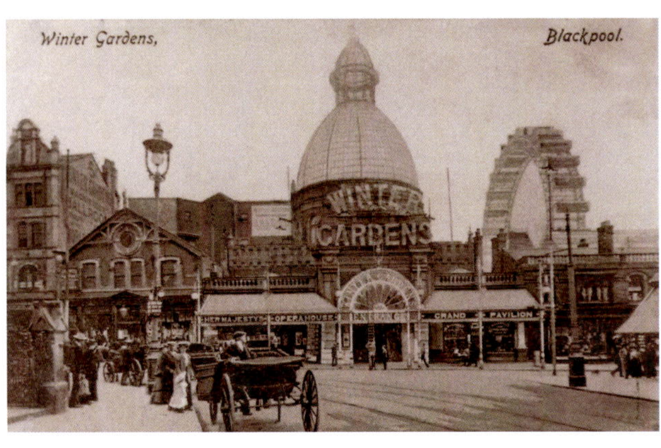

Winter Gardens exterior with Big Wheel.

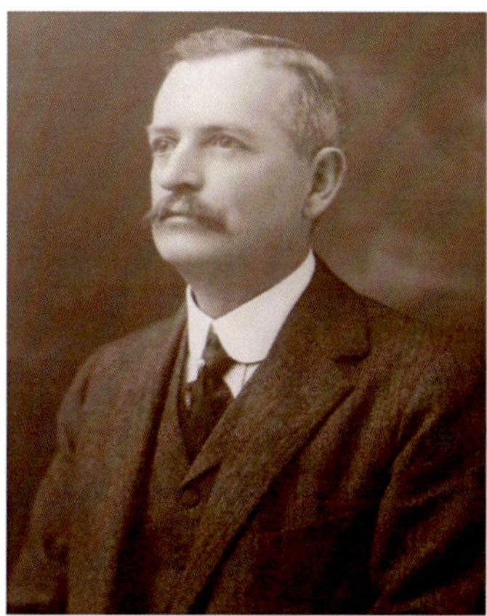 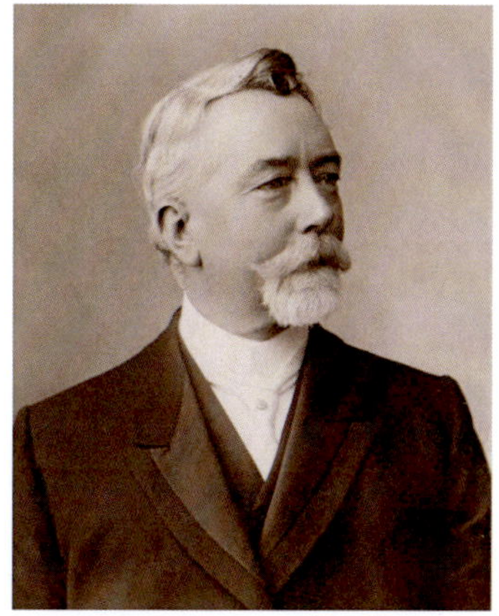

YOUR Colleagues on the Board of Directors of The Blackpool Tower Company, Ltd., and the Officials thereof, who have the privilege of serving under you, feel that the signal honour which has recently been done you by the Corporation of Blackpool in adding your name to the very limited and distinguished roll of Honorary Freemen of this County Borough should be suitably recognised.

As this is also the 'Coming of Age' year both of the Blackpool Tower Company, Ltd., and your Chairmanship, they gladly seize the fitting opportunity of marking these auspicious events in your life by the presentation of this Illuminated Album containing Photographs of your past and present Colleagues, the Chief Officials, and Pictures of the work with which you have been identified, together with a solid Silver Salver.

Your eminent services in the varied high public Offices which you still fill deserve well of the Town of your birth, in the advancement of which you have taken such a deep and lasting interest, and have so freely given of your best energies and means, and we rejoice that the Honorary Freedom of the Borough which has been conferred upon you will give pleasure to you and your family, and will keep your name ever conspicuous and honoured in the remarkable history of progressive Blackpool.

Your Chairmanship of our Company which commenced under great and trying difficulties is consummated in the prosperous condition which obtains to-day. In the early trials which a structure so unique as the Tower and its Buildings naturally encountered, your ever cheerful and optimistic disposition, combined with your dogged determination, financial assistance, and assiduous attention played a very large part in carrying the scheme of construction successfully through and giving to Blackpool a Property which has aided so very materially in the wonderful advancement of this health and pleasure resort.

The development of our Company has been greatly helped by the rare business acumen which you display as Chairman, and in the acquisition of the Palace and Grand Theatre Properties your ripe and unerring judgment was most valuable.

The consolidation of the Company's Finances and the appreciation in value of its securities are due in no small measure to your guidance and steadfastness to the best interests of the Company.

Top left: Robert Parker, John Bickerstaffe's company secretary.

Middle: Tribute to John Bickerstaffe.

Top right: John Bickerstaffe.

Right: John Bickerstaffe memorial inscription.

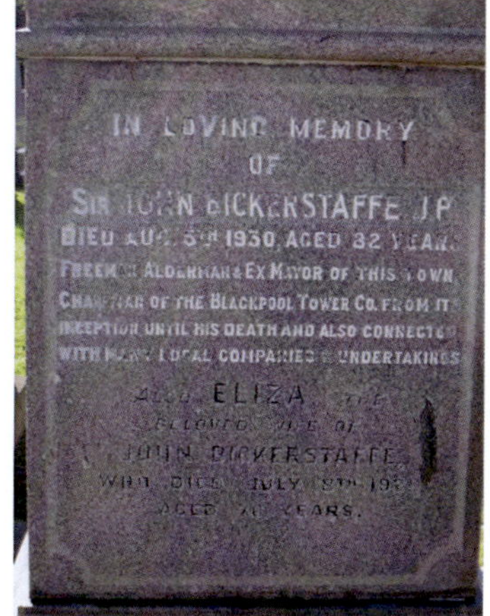

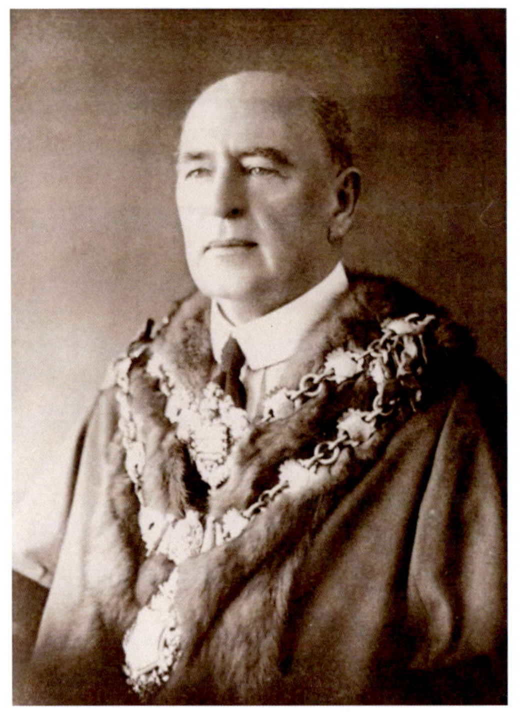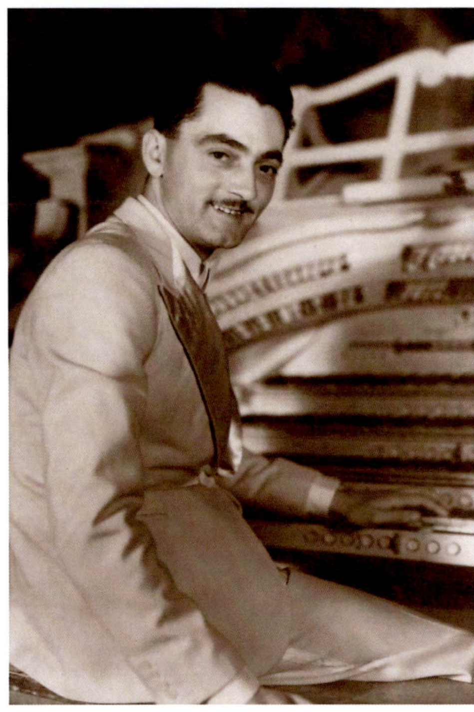

Top left: Mayor Tom Bickerstaffe, *c.* 1925.

Top right: A young Reginald Dixon at the Wurlitzer.

Bottom: The Tower Ballroom after the 1955 fire.

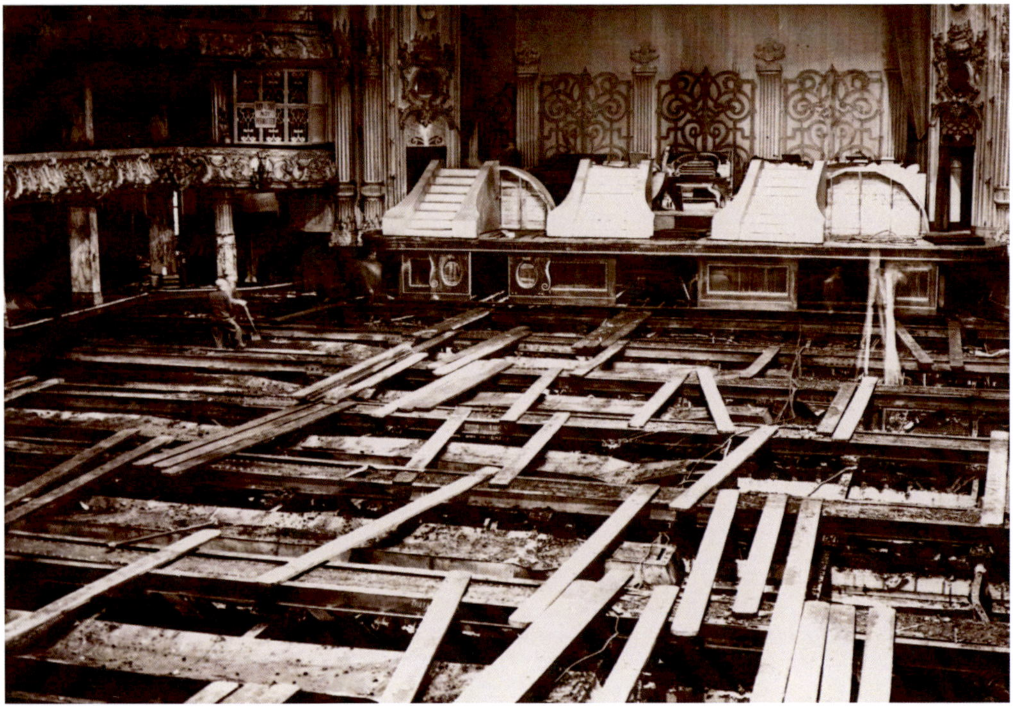

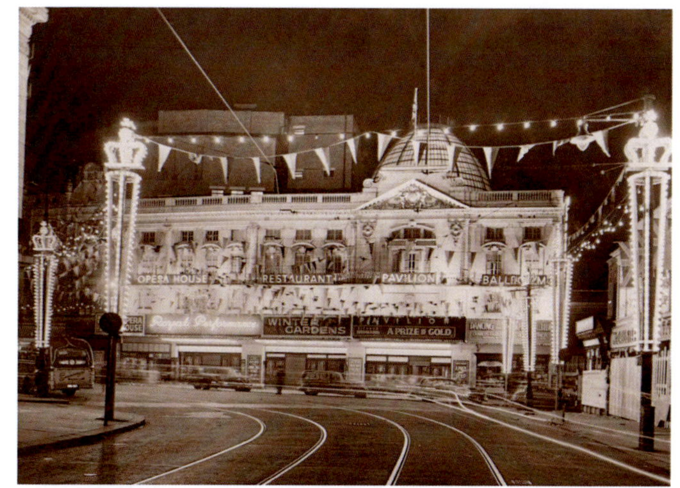

The Royal Variety at the
Opera House, 1955.

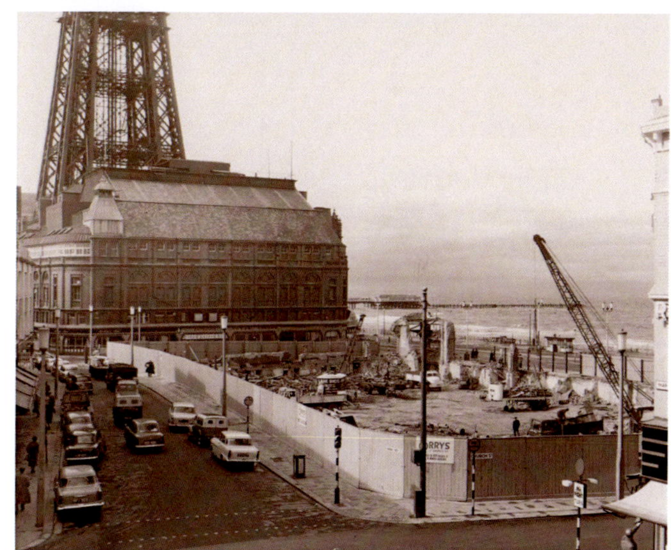

The Palace is
demolished, 1962.

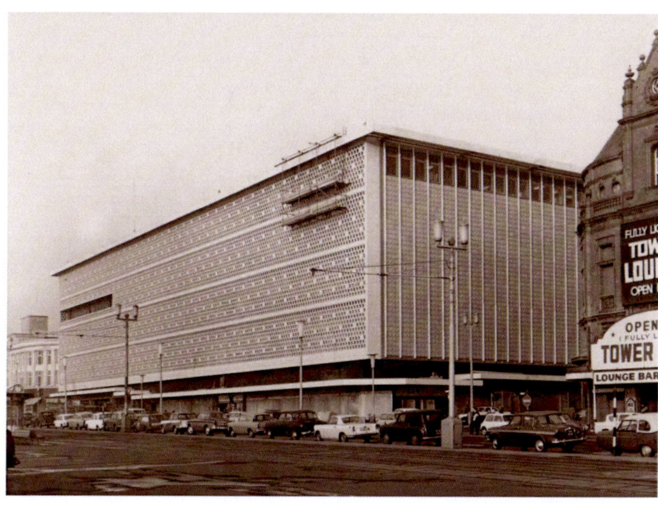

Lewis's store on the
Palace site, 1964.

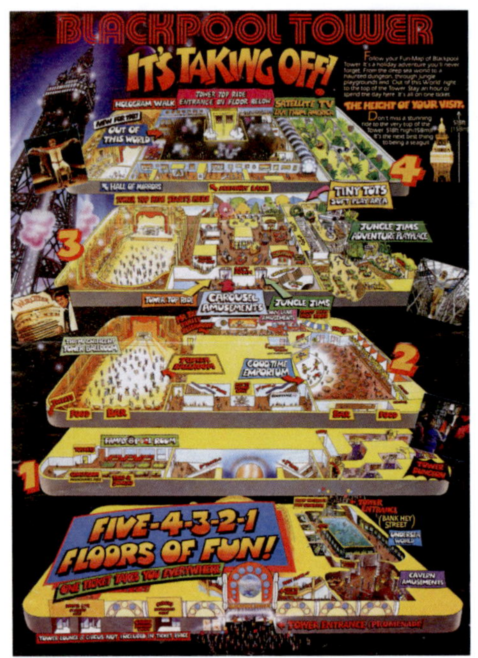

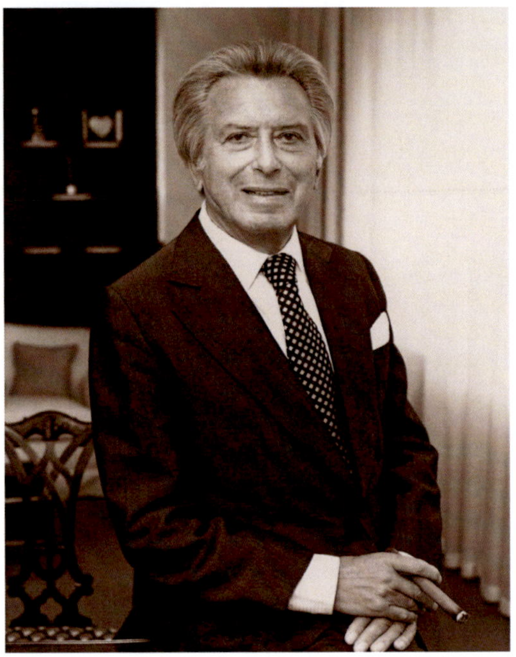

Top left: Flyer shows internal layout of Tower buildings.

Top right: Lord Delfont by Sue Delfont.

Bottom: Billy Marsh, Bernard Delfont, Michael Grade, Leslie Grade and Dennis van Thal at the Café Royal for the sale of London Management by EMI. © Trinity Mirror/ Mirrorpix/Alamy.

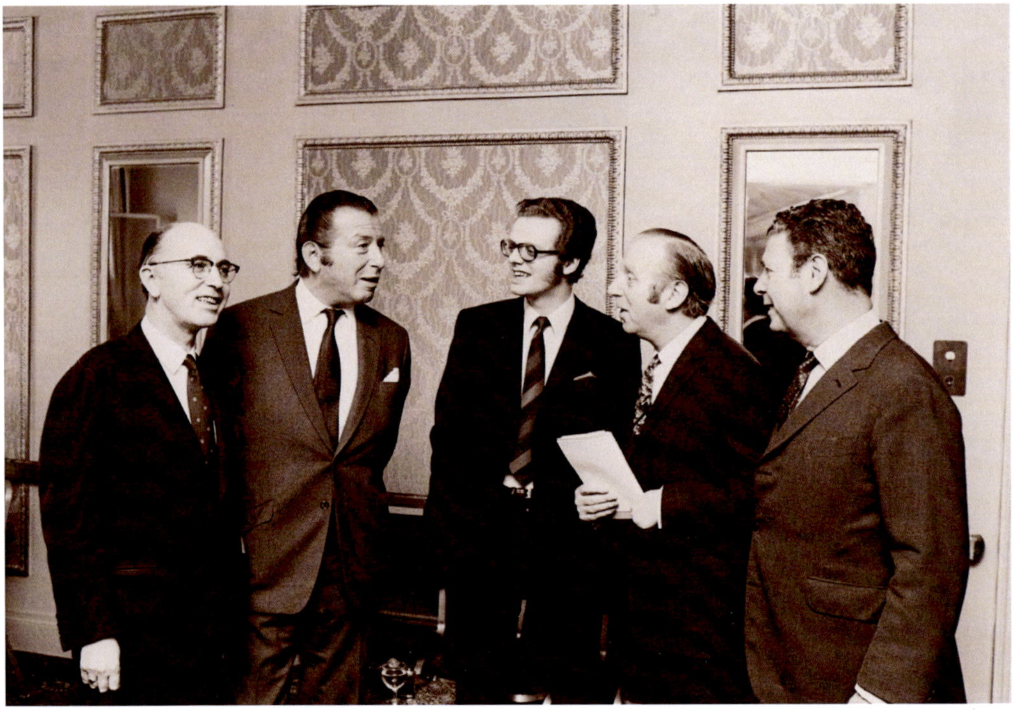

In the event the profits on which they were relying failed to materialise, they reduced the dividend but could not cut it entirely, and dropped the depreciation charge in the accounts, but they were forced to borrow money to enable them to complete. At the 1922 shareholders' meeting Bickerstaffe noted that the company had an overdraft, for the first time for many years. He explained that they had spent £155,761 on acquiring property, and although much of this had been financed out of receipts, the fall off had left them needing to seek support. He added that the Lancashire and Yorkshire Bank had, as ever, been accommodating.

Table 7.1 below shows the evolution of the company's operating profits, analysed across its major operations, over the decade, together with the total profits and the total dividend paid at the end of the year (but excluding the Winter Gardens). The total profit approximates to what would nowadays be called 'operating profit', and would have taxation, interest and transfers to reserves deducted before arriving at the profit available to shareholders, which is why the dividend is systematically a much lower number.

The table illustrates the dip in profits in the early years of the decade, and then the acceleration to new levels from 1925, followed by a reduction in 1930. Curiously the general strike in 1926 seems to have had no effect on business. Bickerstaffe, newly dubbed 'Sir John', commented 'What with strikes and lock-outs, and the scarcity of money in the country, I think we have every reason to be satisfied with the result of the past season's working. It is another proof of the popularity of good old Blackpool.' (*Blackpool Gazette* 7 December 1926).

The table also shows the relative contribution of the additional parts (not the Winter Gardens) that Bickerstaffe added to the company after the war.

Blackpool Tower Co. – Operations

Year	Dividend	Total before tax/int etc.	Tower Profit	Palace Profit	Grand Profit	Central Beach Profit	St Anne's Profit	Lytham Profit
1920	23205	79220	53487	17394	8339			
1921	15191	55898	28535	17872	4537	4954		
1922	15191	48618	24931	12125	6097	5465		
1923	20637	74388	37586	24644	5814	6344		
1924	25691	77235	41141	26717	2710	6667		
1925	32244	85012	43676	31836	4775	7549	-2824	
1926	32670	85642	40296	26475	10075	7395	1401	
1927	44970	111422	60749	35008	7648	7082	935	
1928	67257	112035	70065	27746	7276	6957	-9	
1929	67844	124815	73042	32177	10622	6980	1994	
1930	65797	97014	63609	21701	4076	6578	-552	1602

The table shows that the Tower (including the circus, the ballroom, the ascent of the Tower, bars and restaurants and shops) remained the key money earner for the company. The Palace did start to catch it up however, with its revamped cinema from 1923. The Grand Theatre had variable results, but this is normal. The theatre owner could sometimes rent the theatre to a producer for the summer, but more commonly took a share of receipts, as well as takings from the bars. If the producer's show was a big success, the Tower Co. would benefit, but it would also lose if the show was less popular. The same is also true of the cinema, although it was far less common for a distributor to rent a cinema. The exhibitor virtually always 'rented' the film from the distributor against a percentage of receipts. The percentage would vary with the perceived popularity of the film, but generally the exhibitor would keep at least 50 per cent of the admissions receipts and all the bar and confectionery sales.

In 1925 the Tower Co. bought a property known as St Anne's Palace (St Anne's being the next town to the south of Blackpool) and operated it as a cinema, and in 1930 opened another in the neighbouring town of Lytham. As can be seen the return was relatively small and variable, but then the investment was also relatively small. It can be seen that in this decade Bickerstaffe was expanding the company's involvement in cinema. In 1925 he had told the shareholders that the purchase 'ought to prove very valuable to the company,' even though the internal accounting records show that it made a loss that year (*Blackpool Gazette* 8 December 1925). However, there is not enough detail to know whether the absence of profit in the first year was due to Bickerstaffe's established preferences for immediately upgrading any property he was concerned with, and charging the cost against profit, or lack of public interest in its films.

Knighthood

Bickerstaffe received a knighthood in the King's birthday honours list for 1926, whose publication had been delayed until July as a result of the general strike. The citation for Sir John was for 'political and public services'. The *Gazette* of 3 July 1926 says this was for 'the distinguished part that he has played in Blackpool's development and for his notable service to the district and to the Conservative party.' It adds that he had been chairman and leader of the Conservative party in Blackpool for over twenty years and a member of the borough council for forty-six years. It said he was a Justice of the Peace for the county and for the borough and a freeman of the borough.

Then in his seventies, Sir John was about to achieve the pinnacle of building his entertainments empire in Blackpool. His knighthood was followed two years later by the acquisition of the

Winter Gardens Co., which had been the Tower Company's main rival since it had been launched.

The Winter Gardens Co.

The Blackpool Winter Gardens Co. was formed in 1875 and its main 'pavilion' opened in 1878, in the town centre, some way back from the sea front. The aim was to provide an indoor facility with seating for 2,500 – at this time the preferred style of multi-purpose entertainment facility. A pavilion might typically consist mostly of a large room with a flat dance floor on which seats could be placed in different configurations for concerts or tea-dances or some years later even film shows. It would have a raised stage area on which scenery could be mounted in a static way, but no 'fly tower' above the stage in which scenery could be suspended and dropped onto the stage as required. In many ways it was not dissimilar from school halls or church halls, although a more elaborate layout might include raised seating or boxes round the side, and even a balcony, as in the original Tower Pavilion.

The idea of winter gardens was popular in the latter part of the nineteenth century,[1] and was an attempt to provide entertainment with shelter and warmth when the weather was bad and so that the resort could extend its season. The Blackpool Winter Gardens was built on the site of a large house that was 200 yards or more back from the promenade (and actually quite close to the site of what became the Tower). Turner and Palmer[2] say the Winter Gardens building was magnificent, and bigger than the Free Trade Hall in Manchester. They comment that the aim was to appeal to the more upmarket visitors to Blackpool. An unintended consequence was that the North Pier Co., seeing the threat to their business, constructed an 'Indian Pavilion' on the pier to rival the Winter Gardens.

However, Turner and Palmer say that the Winter Gardens Co. nearly went bankrupt after disastrous seasons in 1879 and 1880, reflecting a major depression throughout the UK economy. The number of middle-class visitors started to fall but at the same time working class people were earning more money, and 'By the mid-1880s Blackpool was becoming an unmistakably working class resort'[3] The Winter Gardens Pavilion initially featured occasional performances of plays or recitals.

After a certain amount of infighting, the company decided to build a theatre next door within the Winter Gardens site, and in 1889 the Opera House, designed by Frank Matcham, was opened with a performance of the Gilbert and Sullivan hit, *The Yeomen of the Guard*. The timing was auspicious because it coincided with the start of a boom period, and the fortunes of the company were much improved. However, there was also no lack of competition: the Grand Theatre opened in 1894 as did the Tower.

The Winter Gardens management encouraged the construction of a Big Wheel (Ferris wheel) as a counter-attraction to the Tower. This opened in 1896 but did not prove particularly popular. It was finally dismantled once the Tower Co. took over. A more successful venture was the construction of the Empress Ballroom within the Winter Gardens site, built on what had started out as an open air roller-skating rink. This opened in 1896 to compete with the Tower, and probably motivated the Tower Co.[4] to upgrade the Tower Pavilion into the Tower Ballroom in 1899, just as it then upgraded the Circus, to compete with the Alhambra circus just starting out next door to the Tower.

There is no doubt that Bickerstaffe was a very competitive person who did not rest on his laurels, and wanted his company to be the most profitable in Blackpool. He even competed with the Winter Gardens to be the first company each year to publish its financial statements and to hold its annual shareholders' meeting. In the local newspapers the Tower Co. result would normally appear a week or two before the other larger companies including the Winter Gardens, the Blackpool Pier Co., the South Jetty Co. and so on. In the early days of the Tower Co. its financial year-end was 30 September, and Bickerstaffe would aim to have its financial statements published by late October and hold the shareholders' meeting early in November. It then paid the dividend to shareholders before Christmas, and the business went into hibernation for the off season.

Today, with the benefit of sophisticated computer software, a company could reckon to have a draft set of statements available within a week of the year-end, but will then spend a long time checking for outstanding charges, resolving queries, deciding the dividend, estimating taxation etc. A large multinational might publish its statements in five to six weeks after the year-end. Smaller companies in the UK are allowed nine months to finalise their figures. The rapidity of the Tower Co.'s finalisation of its figures is astonishing, and implies that the accounting staff were well on top of their systems, and that Bickerstaffe made quick decisions on strategic issues such as maintenance reserves, other transfers to reserves, and later taxation.

The Tower Co. having quickly disposed of what could have been one major competitor, the Alhambra Co., the Winter Gardens remained the largest local competitor, and it can be little surprise that Bickerstaffe called the acquisition of the Winter Gardens 'One of the finest moves made in Blackpool' (*Gazette* 11 February 1928). The 'hostile' takeover of the company started in late 1927 with a rebuff by the Winter Gardens board to Mrs Frieda Huddlestone[5], who held 10,000 shares (nearly 10 per cent of the issued capital) in the Winter Gardens, which had been left to her by her husband, a former managing director of the company. However, its antecedents went much further back.

At the 1928 annual meeting of the company, the resigning chairman, Charles Hardman, said that as early as 1912 one of the directors of the Winter Gardens, F. A. Badman[6], had approached the Tower Co. and negotiated a deal where the latter would offer five of its £1 Ordinary shares for one £5 Ordinary share in the Winter Gardens. At the time the Tower shares were trading at above the face value and the Winter Gardens at below face value, so the offer represented an interesting premium. However, the then chairman refused to sanction the deal, and the board of directors eventually voted it down formally.

Nothing more was done until the 1920s. The then chairman, John Huddlestone, died in July 1925. Mr Hardman said the board had had to take over the management of the company and found its premises in a state of disrepair and its operations poorly controlled. They had had to close some loss-making operations and boost others, as well as replacing furniture and equipment. He reported that in November 1925 he had received a letter from Mrs Huddlestone suggesting that she and Charles Badman (who had inherited a similarly large interest from his father) should be appointed to the board, 'by reason of their large holding'. The board had refused, arguing that they were reorganising the company and Mrs Huddlestone would most likely be embarrassed at the criticisms of her husband she would probably hear.

Sue Arthur[7] writes that two years' later 'James Grandidge, another major shareholder of the company, quietly approached Sir John Bickerstaffe in the autumn of 1927 seeking a merger of the two Companies'. She says that Grandidge, Badman and Huddlestone between them held 25,000 of the 105,000 Winter Gardens shares in issue at the time.

The result of this was a formal offer letter from Bickerstaffe to Winter Gardens shareholders on 18 January 1928 offering them a straight exchange of one Tower Co. share for one Winter Gardens share (they had by then been split to have a £1 face value as well). This was revealed under the headline 'The Tower – Winter Gardens Sensation' in the *Gazette* of 21 January 1928, where it was also announced that 58,647 shareholders had already accepted the offer.

The *Gazette* said it had been briefed by a 'prominent official' of the Tower Co. They had been told that several disaffected shareholders of the Winter Gardens Co. had approached the Tower Co. after publication of its 1927 results. Discussions had taken place over several weeks in December and had been followed by taking Counsel's opinion. Holders of 43,320 Winter Gardens shares had indicated they would accept the offer, and a formal letter was drawn up and sent to all Winter Gardens shareholders.

The Tower Co., said the *Gazette*, had reassured it that the Tower Co.'s motivation was only to achieve for Blackpool 'the best possible in the amusement world'. To the possible criticism that the Tower Co. would reduce the entertainment on offer, the company pointed to its acquisition of the Alhambra and then the Grand Theatre, claiming that these had been followed by an improvement in what was offered.

The article reproduces the 18 January offer letter to Winter Gardens shareholders which points out that holders of 43,320 shares had already indicated approval as well noting that the last quoted price on the Manchester stock exchange of their respective shares before the offer was: Tower Co. 53s (£2-13-0 or £2.65) and Winter Gardens 42/6 (£2-2-6 or £2.12) or a premium of nearly 25 per cent.

It also set out the pattern of dividends in recent years:

	1923	1924	1925	1926	1927
Tower Co.	8 per cent	10 per cent	12½ per cent	12½ per cent	17½ per cent
Winter Gardens Co.	7½ per cent	5 per cent	5 per cent	7½ per cent	10 per cent

The letter asserted that if the Tower Co. obtained a controlling interest it was certain that it could increase the profitability of the Winter Gardens. It included a form of commitment to accept the proposal, which also bound the shareholder to vote against any increase in the capital of the Winter Gardens or any sale of its assets before the transfer went through. This presumably was the result of the legal advice they had received: two standard ways to foil a hostile takeover are (a) to issue new shares to a 'white knight' rescuer which would have the effect of reducing the proportion of shares held by the dissident shareholders, and (b) to sell off the principal assets to another company so as to make the takeover pointless.

The offer was conditional upon approval by Tower shareholders of the scheme. On 8 February there was a special meeting of the Tower shareholders to approve the increase in capital necessary and the issue of 105,000 ordinary shares in exchange for Winter Gardens shares. Alderman Broadhead, a director of the Tower Co., said it was going to be 'an era of peace and prosperity'.

The board enumerated the advantages of the deal. They said that the land on which the Winter Gardens was built was still in the books at its original (1875) purchase price and was worth much more than that at current prices; the share capital was relatively small and should yield a good return; its debenture had been issued at the low rate of 4 per cent, well below the current market rate; and the company had a fine range of buildings and related licences. However they warned that the Winter Gardens Company's properties were 'not up to the standard' of the Tower properties and it would take some time and expenditure to bring them up to the mark.

They added that in the past the Winter Gardens management and the Tower management had been in competition to attract the best entertainers, but once under a unified management they would no longer be bidding against each other and should be able to obtain better prices. They also noted that both companies had extensive catering activities which, if combined, would enable them to negotiate better terms with suppliers on the basis of increased volume. They observed that it would also have been possible for the Winter Gardens to be taken over by a much larger company, which could have had severe consequences for the Tower Co. They commented that with the two companies combined they could 'successfully compete with all-comers'.

Bickerstaffe at the end of the meeting told shareholders that he and his children held securities with a nominal value of £27,568 in the Tower Co. and they could be sure that he would not recommend anything to them that was not in the company's best interests. 'I am perfectly satisfied that it will be a success, not only to the Tower Co. but to the Winter Gardens Co. as well,' he said.

While the shareholders collectively own a company, they do not actually have any executive authority over the company's activities. The people responsible for making decisions and appointing managers are the directors, who are elected by shareholders at the annual meeting. The shareholders 'control' the company because they can hire and fire the directors, but this can only be done collectively by vote in a shareholders' meeting.

When one company takes over another, the directors of the acquired company, if they want to keep their jobs, can normally be expected to cooperate with the directors of the acquiring company. For example, a board usually has the power to appoint new directors on a temporary basis until the next annual meeting, so they will appoint representatives of the new owner who will be formally elected at the next annual meeting. The new owner can then go ahead and make any management changes.

In the case of the Winter Gardens Co., the acquisition of its shares by the Tower Co. was a hostile takeover which the directors of the Winter Gardens had opposed. It had been done with the connivance of two shareholders whom the Winter Gardens directors had refused to appoint to their board. The Tower Co. quickly received enough acceptances to take control – more than 75 per cent of the shares in fact, which meant they could not only appoint directors but change the statutes of the company if they wished. However, the directors of the Winter Gardens Co. refused to appoint new directors or stand down.

This meant that the Tower Co. could not step in and start to manage the properties for the 1928 season. Instead it had no option but to call a special meeting of Winter Gardens shareholders at which it sacked the existing board and appointed new directors in a very public way. Given the need for the Tower Company's ownership of the shares to be registered by the Winter Gardens Co. secretary, and then for a formal notice period to elapse, the big showdown did not take place until the middle of May, by which point the Tower Co. held 90,466 of the 105,000 shares in issue. The *Gazette* of 14 May carried the subheading 'Vigorous Comments at Special Meeting of Shareholders' and 'some hard hitting'.

About to become ex-chairman of the Winter Gardens Co., Charles Hardman, told the shareholders that the board was very disappointed that it had not been allowed to see through the improvements that it had started in 1925. The motion before the meeting was to dismiss the existing board and replace them with the Tower Co.'s nominees 'with the view of vesting the management and control of that company in the directors of the Blackpool Tower Co.'. Mr Hardman said it had been suggested that the board should resign, but they were not prepared to do it. There had been no reason given: they had not been accused of being dishonest or of being incapable of conducting the affairs of the company. They felt it was only right that they should give an account of their stewardship and show there was no valid reason whatever why the board should be discharged. He said he had been a shareholder for forty years and a director for twenty and had 'given of my best to ensure prosperity and success to the company.'

He related that he had had to act as a guarantor for the company's overdraft, which at the start of the season could be £40,000 – 'being a guarantor was not exactly a bed of roses'. He went on to relate the unconsummated proposal of 1912, then the episode in 1924 and 1925 when shareholders were unhappy with the performance of the management. But they had engaged a new manager in 1926 and were happy with what he had done. He said the theatre had been raised from third rate to first rate, and a new band engaged for the Empress Ballroom.

He went on to talk about Mrs Huddlestone's letter and queried why, if they were dissatisfied with the board they had not done what the Tower Co. had subsequently done and called a special meeting of shareholders. What arguments had been used to persuade any sensible body of men to enter into such an amalgamation, he could not imagine. It was a bad business arrangement to start with. It was a financial disaster for the company and was not good for the town of Blackpool in general. He said the Tower Co. was taking over for £105,000 of shares assets that were worth at least half a million. 'Talk about sacrificing your birthright for a mess of pottage! I do not think there was ever a more glorious example than this!'

Mr Hardman said that the two boards had in fact met in April, when it had been suggested the present directors should resign and be replaced by Alderman Tom Bickerstaffe, Mrs Huddlestone, Mr Charles Badman and Mr Robert Parker (the company secretary of the Tower Co.). No fifth director had been proposed but he imagined it would be Mr Grandidge. He said the Winter Gardens directors thought it was contrary to the interests of the Winter Gardens Co. to put its management in the hands of these people who were 'quite unacquainted with the affairs of the Company, its business arrangements and its working.' He added that if the existing board members were to be removed, then they would have to be removed by formal vote, they would not resign.

Two other directors then addressed the meeting, and after about an hour the motion to dismiss the old directors and install the four new ones was put to the vote. Sir John Bickerstaffe requested a count of shares voted as opposed to a show of hands. The result was:

Votes in favour   98,750
Votes against   1,048

Within a week, the new Winter Gardens board had met, and installed Harry Hall, general manager of the Tower Co., in overall charge of the Winter Gardens as well. The *Gazette* reported on 17 May that Mr Hutchinson, who had managed the Winter Gardens since 1926, had 'by an amicable and mutually satisfactory arrangement' agreed to this and promised his cooperation during the period of reorganisation. More staff changes were announced two weeks' later and from the beginning of June, where previously the Tower Co. and the Winter Gardens had each taken half page advertisements in each issue of the local papers, this dropped to a single half page, advertising the entertainment at both sites.[8]

On 2 June the *Gazette* announced that the Big Wheel was to turn no more. The paper reported that the Tower Co. had called for an engineer's report, and on the basis of that 'they could not justify the continuance of its use owing to the condition of the structure.' They added that the costs of putting the wheel into a suitable condition would mean that it was not profitable to run.

This announcement had caused alarm because it was the start of the season, and people had stocked up on postcards of Blackpool that included the Big Wheel. The Tower Co. had therefore agreed not to start to dismantle the wheel until after the end of the season, during which retailers could run down their stocks. The *Gazette* reporter noted that the wheel had run since 1896 without any accidents – except that one night the staff had shut it down while inadvertently leaving one family marooned in a cabin for the night.

Death of John Bickerstaffe

Bickerstaffe died on the evening of Tuesday 5 August 1930, at the age of eighty-two. The newspapers report that he had been taken ill in June, but was believed to be recovering and had put in an appearance at a prize-giving late in July. However, he had a heart attack on the Monday night, and died late on the following day.

Nearly 100,000 holiday makers lined the route of his funeral, according to the *West Lancashire Evening Gazette*: 'The crowded promenade was hushed in poignant grief as the procession passed along the windswept road along which he had so often walked, and in front of the Tower and the Palace, amusement centres he did so much to create.'

The newspaper added that 'a generation died – a generation of sand dunes and white-walled fishermen's cottages – when John Bickerstaffe passed to his rest.' The *Blackpool Gazette* commented that the rise of John Bickerstaffe paralleled the rise of Blackpool. He was born at Hounds Hill on 20 January 1848. He became a member of the Town Council in 1880, at the age of thirty-two. He was elected an Alderman in 1887 and served two years as mayor from 1889 to 1891.

The paper said that from the time of the construction of the Tower 'Alderman John was in the thick of almost all developments in a Blackpool that was developing like wildfire. His breezy optimism infected his colleagues, and his robust imperialism and Conservatism attuned well with the spirit of the times.' He was made a Justice of the Peace in 1905 and a freeman of Blackpool in 1912. He made substantial donations to the Victoria Hospital and to the Church of England Victoria schools in Blackpool. He also gave land to Blackpool Council to create a park.

Sir John's directorships and interests in local businesses had been numerous. He had been a director of the Blackpool Electric Tramway Co. (one of the earliest to provide a tram service), Raikes Hall Estate Ltd., and the Blackpool Passenger Steamboat Co. He is reported as having sold virtually all his holdings during the darkest days of the Tower Co. when it was still under construction and its shares were selling for less than half their face value. Bickerstaffe had put all his money into buying Tower shares to try to support the share price. He was still a director of the Clifton Hotel Co. and the Crystal Mineral Water Co., according to the *Gazette*.

In a piece in the *Gazette* (9 August 1930), an anonymous writer wrote:

> He was brave, he was courageous. He would advocate a million-pound promenade or the spending of thousands of pounds on the town's improvements as courageously as he tackled his many private enterprises. He may not have laid the foundation stone of Blackpool, but he had much to do with the building of the edifice.

The Company Secretary of the Tower Co. during most of John Bickerstaffe's reign had been Robert Parker. He wrote a piece in the *Blackpool Gazette* of 31 March 1934 in which he said 'I was probably in closer business relationship with Sir John than anybody else, and am, therefore, well able to review his work'. He had first met Bickerstaffe in 1885, when as a junior in the equivalent of an accounting firm, he was deputed to take minutes at the Tramway Co. He eventually joined the Tower Co. in 1897.

He commented: 'In every transaction that was undertaken, John Bickerstaffe was animated by one ideal only – the success of the company of which he was rightly so proud. His close examination of every detail thoroughly impressed you also with the necessity of mastering in advance of everything likely to come before him, and so he instilled in you that thoroughness that had made him all he was.' Parker says Bickerstaffe was also firm – 'that firmness was grafted into him during the early and difficult days of the Tower's history.'

Another long-serving staff member also has insights to offer on the management culture at the Tower Co. Bernard Crabtree joined the Tower Co. in 1933 as an office boy, and retired in 1981 as entertainments manager. While he joined after John Bickerstaffe's death, the culture of the company when he arrived would have been that which had been instilled by the first chairman. Crabtree writes[9] 'It was a very profitable business and, although not the most generous of employers, there was considerable prestige in working for them.'

As an example of the company's down to earth parsimoniousness, Crabtree gives the example of being sent to the ladies' toilets to free women accidentally locked in a cubicle. In those days it was common to have to put a (pre-decimalisation) penny into the door of a cubicle to gain access (the origin of the expression 'spending a penny'). Crabtree says that sometimes women in a hurry and not having a penny would put in a half-crown (about the same size but worth 30 pennies) which gave them access, but jammed the machine so they could not get out. In his early days with the company, working at the Palace, Crabtree was sent to open up the slot mechanism and take out the half crown. However, he did not return it to the client, but kept one penny and gave back only 29, as the company considered it had earned its penny.

Crabtree was soon promoted to working as a junior assistant in the publicity office, then run by Clem Butson. The company evidently believed in internal development and promotion because in time he worked his way up to being in charge of publicity, and from there in 1955 to be deputy to the entertainments manager. At that time the manager was Kathleen Williams, who herself had previously been the secretary to the previous entertainments manager. Crabtree succeeded her in 1960 and held the post for twenty years.

He says that it was company policy before the Second World War that junior employees spent a day each week at one of the company's venues to gain management experience. In Crabtree's case, when he was a junior in the publicity department he would often spend a day at the Grand Theatre. There he would typically help cash up the previous day's takings and then bank them. In the evening he would act as front of house manager. The manager of the Grand also had responsibility for the Opera House.

It can be concluded that the company had a good policy of staff development and employees stayed with it for very long periods. The investment in staff training may, of course, have meant that salaries were a little lower, because the company was not always competing in the market place. But it would also provide a pool of experienced people who could easily cover for each other. The company certainly seemed capable of generating loyalty.

In fact Crabtree implies that loyalty was a valued attribute with more than one side to it. He recounts that after the Second World War, Clem Butson, who by then had risen to be general manager of the Tower Co., left to work for Tom Arnold. Arnold was a well-known and successful London-based show producer who during the war had staged a succession of shows and pantomimes at Tower Co. theatres, but after he poached Clem Butson, he was given no further theatre contracts by the company.

8

SUCCESSION AND DEPRESSION: THE 1930s

When John Bickerstaffe died, he left behind the dominant company in Blackpool entertainment, which he had built up from just the original Tower idea to a successful cash machine that generated good dividends to its investors, and was to be the face of Blackpool entertainment during the resort's golden years from 1930 to 1960. Bickerstaffe's successors as chairman of the company, his brother, his son and his nephew, would continue to exploit the assets and develop them, but would not undertake any major expansion into new entertainment assets. John Bickerstaffe had built the cash machine, his family would keep it running successfully, but not change it substantially.

When Tom Bickerstaffe took over as chairman, he presided over a transition where cinema would become more important thanks to the arrival of sound in 1929, where dance bands became a major attraction at the company's three ballrooms, and radio broadcasts helped to build the resort's reputation and attract ever more visitors. The Wurlitzer organ, installed in 1929 in the Tower Ballroom (and replaced in 1935 with an even grander version) would also become a major attraction in the hands of Reginald Dixon, who continued to make radio broadcasts from the Tower Ballroom until the 1960s, apart from the Second World War.

The company underwent two changes of leadership in this decade. Tom Bickerstaffe, the younger brother of John, took over from him as chairman in 1930. Tom was twelve years' younger than John, but had grown up steeped in the Blackpool entertainment business (they had a third brother who ran a large hardware store in Blackpool). He followed John onto the Blackpool Council in 1891, and like him, was subsequently elected an alderman and also served as mayor (in 1926). As John Walton[1] notes, people from the entertainment industry had a dominant influence on the Blackpool Council, and adds that 'private enterprise worked alongside pubic investment, helping to create Blackpool's attractive image in the outside world' (p86).

Tom Bickerstaffe served as chairman of the council's advertising committee for thirty years. It was at the time an innovation for a town council to have a structure for promoting its facilities to the rest of the country. Blackpool was the first town in the country to do this, although it is now commonplace. John and Tom were therefore both prominent in the council's affairs, while also playing very significant roles in the town's business as a resort. Tom Bickerstaffe is credited with having come up with the idea of the Blackpool Illuminations. This is now a national institution, and consists of extensive displays of coloured lights along the promenade of Blackpool which are a focus for visitors in October each year. Their commercial function is to extend the holiday season – to provide a reason to spend time in Blackpool when it is too cold or wet (or both) to contemplate normal seaside holiday activities there.

At a celebration of the lights in 1973, the chairman of the council said: 'A genius walked in the moonlight sixty years ago – and Blackpool's autumn tills have been ringing happily ever since.' The story is that in 1912 Alderman Tom Bickerstaffe was walking along the promenade with an electrical engineer, looking at the innovative electric street lighting. As they walked he had the idea that they might as well string a few coloured lights along the promenade. This was done and it was observed that people stopped to admire the lights. Bickerstaffe realised that the idea could be developed, and it has become another of Blackpool's unique institutions.

John and Tom Bickerstaffe worked closely together. Tom was appointed a director of the Tower Co. in 1911, and became chairman of the Winter Gardens Co. when that was taken over. Indeed, his obituary in the *Manchester Guardian* (13 February 1934) says that Tom was 'the chief mover' in the acquisition of the Winter Gardens. In as far as he was also a shareholder in the Winter Gardens Co., owning around 2 per cent of its capital, it would be natural that the disgruntled shareholders in that company should turn to him in the first place, rather than go directly to John, but there is no clear evidence one way or the other.

Their father, Robert Bickerstaffe, had been active in the South Jetty Co., and of course, owned the Wellington Hotel. He also operated paddle steamers from the South Pier. The eldest son, John, gradually took over management of these interests, but it is likely that as he fought to keep the Tower financed and sold his other local holdings to generate cash, his brother Tom became the prime mover in these investments. Tom did indeed run the paddle steamer business, although the popularity of these sea trips had dropped off by the 1930s.

The *Manchester Guardian* commented: 'No man knew better what appealed to the holiday crowd.' He was also a director of the Belle Vue entertainment centre in Manchester. Its obituary said: 'His wide experience of the show business proved of immediate value to that undertaking'. Sue Arthur[2] credits him with being innovative, and very outspoken on the subject of relaxation of legal constraints such as licensing hours. At that time bars had to close at 10 p.m. and there were considerable constraints on what entertainment could be offered on a Sunday.

Tom Bickerstaffe died on 12 February 1934. The papers report that he had been attending a meeting at the Grand Hotel in Manchester and was waiting for the train to Blackpool when he collapsed and was taken to hospital, where he died. As Arthur notes, very unusually he had specified that he was to be cremated (which was only possible in Manchester at that time). Unlike his brother, there was therefore no funeral procession through Blackpool, although the lifeboat crew took his ashes out to sea and scattered them there.

Robert Parker, the Tower Co. Secretary, in his 1934 article in the *Gazette* said that Tom was another who had inherited the Bickerstaffe commercial instincts, and in an even more pronounced degree. He was however entirely different in manner from John: 'you had to get used to his ruggedness.' However Parker observed that he was 'characteristically a good listener' and did not express himself until he was fully conversant with the business.

Parker said he worked together with Tom Bickerstaffe on many matters, culminating in the acquisition of the Winter Gardens. He then played a very important part in the development of the Winter Gardens. 'Time and thought – any old hours – were applied with that thoroughness which seemed to get stronger as he got older.' Parker added: 'He gave his mind and body little rest, and never complained. He always reported fit.' Parker had been minded to suggest to the chairman that he should slow down. 'I doubt, however, if any warning would have altered his methods in the slightest. So our company lost a second great chairman.'

With the benefit of hindsight, Parker's words were timely: the company had in effect come to the end of its growth stage. Marketing uses a life cycle analysis for products that divides a product's life into four stages: introduction, growth, maturity and decline, and this model can be used as an analogy for the life of the Blackpool Tower Co. With the passing of Tom Bickerstaffe, the Tower Co. had reached the end of its growth stage. Under John Bickerstaffe the company had built the Tower in its introduction stage, and then, with the help of his brother, during its growth stage had acquired the Grand Theatre, the Palace, and finally the Winter Gardens. It had also expanded into cinemas along the coast.

However, the acquisition of the Winter Gardens was the last piece of significant growth. After 1930 the company continued to keep its premises up to date, but did not invest in any new activities, nor attempt to extend its reach beyond Blackpool. At that point the company entered maturity, and continued to generate profits – it became a 'cash cow' – until the start of its decline, which probably coincided with the arrival of television in the mid-1950s and could be marked by the closure of the Palace at the end of that decade.

The New Chairman

When Sir John died, his seat on the board had been taken by his son Robert Gerard Bickerstaffe ('Robert Jnr'). John Bickerstaffe had fathered eight children, but only one son, born in 1875. Robert Jnr had chosen to leave Blackpool and practised as a solicitor in Liverpool. Nonetheless he joined the board when he inherited his father's shareholdings, and succeeded Tom as chairman in 1934, holding that office until 1947, when he was seventy.

Parker commented 'in education he has, of course, a great advantage over both [his father and his uncle] ... his knowledge of Blackpool is lifelong. He certainly has no similar municipal experience, but personally I think, in these days in all events, it may prove an advantage for our directors to have no official connection with municipal life.'

Parker continued: 'Mr Robert's three and a half years' training on our board under his uncle has been very helpful, and I feel as the years pass he will fully develop that business acumen typical of the two late chairmen, and so necessary to maintain the stability and progress of our companies.'

An article in the *Blackpool Gazette* at the time Robert Gerard Bickerstaffe became chairman noted: 'Having lived and worked unostentatiously in Liverpool for many years, Mr Robert Bickerstaffe is not widely known here.' The newspaper added: 'Those who remember him as a young man recall a singularly charming disposition, and his legal and business knowledge should be of value to the big business that he will now assist to direct' (31 March 1934).

Although both John and Tom Bickerstaffe had been prominent in Blackpool business and municipal circles, and spent a good deal of time at the company's premises, they did not deal with the day to day management of the company, relying on the key person of the general manager, with an able and loyal support staff. Consequently when Robert Bickerstaffe took over, the company continued to run effectively under its full time management, but was no longer involved with municipal affairs, and there was no further expansion of its activities.

Company Performance

The period between the two World Wars was marked by economic instability across the developed world, not least because of the government debts that had accumulated during the First World War. Nevertheless some countries experienced a boom in the early 1920s, which exacerbated the slump in demand that followed. A fall in demand in the United States in the late 1920s led to a fall of national income of almost 30 per cent between 1929 and 1933[3], helping to move the world economy into a downward spiral which was made worse by attempts by individual countries to protect their economies with trade barriers and quotas. The UK had been slower to recover from the War, but it too suffered a major depression, with unemployment as high as 25 per cent in northern England, the Tower Company's prime catchment area. With the benefit of hindsight, the takeover of the Winter Gardens Co. in 1928 was badly timed in that the economy moved into recession in 1929 and stayed there until the mid-1930s.

**Table 8.1 Blackpool Tower Co. annual profits
(as reported in published financial statements)**

Year	Net profit	Earnings Per share
	£	£
1927	85,250	0.28
1928	92,153	0.22
1929	95,571	0.23
1930	91,912	0.22
1931	85,207	0.21
1932	85,094	0.21
1933	80,337	0.19
1934	103,433	0.25
1935	113,975	0.28
1936	124,397	0.30
1937	128,402	0.31
1938	96,002	0.23
1939	28,825	0.07

Nonetheless the Tower Co. proved itself reasonably resilient, although the dip in performance was masked somewhat by having acquired the Winter Gardens. The two companies in aggregate made more than the Tower Co. on its own, but less individually than they had previously. Table 8.1 shows an approximate earnings per share figure (net profits divided by shares in issue) to illustrate this. It shows that while the total profit reported by the Tower Co. increased in 1928 and 1929, this included the profit of the Winter Gardens. Having issued 105,000 shares to buy the Winter Gardens Co., the total profit thereafter had to be divided among more shareholders. This is demonstrated by the earnings per share, which were £0.28 in 1927 and fell consistently from 1928 to 1933, only reaching £0.28 again in 1935.

The figures should be interpreted with a certain amount of caution, because companies always have some expenditure which can be deferred or accelerated. As discussed in earlier chapters, the company had stopped charging depreciation on the Tower and buildings in 1921, and started doing so again in 1935. This meant that the 1935 financial statements showed an expense of £10,000 which had no counterpart in the 1934 figures. While it made charges in 1936, 1937and 1938, there was no charge in the disastrous 1939 year.

Turner and Palmer[4] say that by comparison with the rapid development previously, there was little or no private investment in the resort at this period. To an extent the Tower Co. was an exception in that once it took over the Winter Gardens in 1928 it set out to improve and renovate its facilities, in line with its established policy of continuously updating and upgrading the entertainments. Tom Bickerstaffe announced at the 1931 shareholders' meeting that three years of work on the Winter Gardens were at an end, saying: 'The property as a whole is now in an up-to-date condition, [the directors] do not anticipate spending further money on capital account for some years to come.' The upgrade had included installing cinema projection equipment with sound at the Winter Gardens, as well as building the Olympia exhibition hall on the site of the former Big Wheel, and installing a suite of Spanish-themed interiors.

The Arrival of Radio

The arrival of talking pictures was something that would dominate the evolution of Blackpool during this decade, but it was also much affected by the arrival of another technological innovation – radio. One of the major innovators was Marconi, who started a radio station to broadcast to the public. The problem in the 1920s, as also later with different technology, was that although the hardware was developing quickly, especially with the arrival of the radio valve, there was a dearth of content. A consortium of manufacturers got together in 1922 to form a broadcaster, the British Broadcasting Company, which was to produce programmes that could be received on the radio sets they manufactured. The government decided after some reflection that the broadcaster should be under public control and the British Broadcasting Corporation (BBC) was given its charter in 1927.

Radio sets were not cheap, but crystal sets, on which someone could listen on headphone could be easily assembled at home (I had one as a child in the 1950s), and radios rapidly became cheaper as demand grew. The demand depended on the BBC (and private commercial stations) putting out material that people wanted to listen to, and on technological developments which meant that nationwide broadcasting was feasible in the early 1930s. Radio was another innovation in entertainment that the Tower Co. was able to harness to its advantage. The BBC needed content, and the Tower Co. had it in the form of the dance bands at its three ballrooms (Empress, Tower and Palace), and its Wurlitzer organ. The musicians were paid by the Tower Co., so the cost to the BBC was minimal (that would change), and for the Tower Co. the broadcasts were a national advertisement.

The Wurlitzer had been installed in the Tower Ballroom in 1929 but proved initially difficult to handle until a young organist called Reginald Dixon presented himself for audition. Dixon was a cinema organist from Sheffield, whose career was about to reach an early end with the introduction of talking pictures. He was therefore looking for a new opening, and found it at the Tower. He was able to master the Wurlitzer, and was even so successful that he was able to persuade the Tower Co. to install a new one in 1935 with modifications to meet his precise requirements.

Reg Dixon became a fixture at the Tower, and also on the *BBC Light Programme* (the forerunner of Radio Two). People danced to his playing in the ballroom and the BBC broadcast regular recitals by him. He became a fixture at the Tower and on the radio. He did not retire until 1970 and became a permanent part of the Tower's image, and that of Blackpool generally.

His signature tune was 'I do like to be beside the sea-side'. His recordings are still available.

New Chairman

As the figures show, 1933 was the lowest point of the depression for the Tower Co., and business started to build up again from 1934. However, the year started badly for the company with the death of Tom Bickerstaffe. Robert Bickerstaffe now took over from his uncle, even though he had no direct link with the entertainment world. Notwithstanding, 1934 was a better year for profits and 1935 was more so, allowing the company to increase its reserves, and leaving it with a significant cash pile, in the absence of new capital expenditure or improvement programmes.

In its earliest years the company had, of course, been desperately short of finance. The Tower had been completed only because John Bickerstaffe had been able to raise funds through preference shares and then a debenture. Even by the end of the 1890s the company was still financed in roughly equal parts with debt and equity. By 1935 the situation was quite different: equity (see table) had risen from 50 per cent of total finance to 75 per cent. What should the company do in these circumstances?

Had John Bickerstaffe still been at the helm, it might have looked to buy or build another entertainment facility, but under his son, the decision was taken to redeem the £220,000 of debentures which had played such an important role in the company's survival and then expansion: in other words it decided on financial consolidation not expansion. This underlines that the company had gone from being an aggressive, expanding business to a settled one concentrating on generating cash flows from its existing operations.

At the end of 1935 the balance sheet showed £138,046 of cash, and this was used, together with the cash generated in 1936 to pay off the debenture – an overdraft of £29,696 was also necessary but had been paid off by the end of 1937. The effect of this was to take equity up to 90 per cent of total financing, meaning that from an investor perspective the company had gone from low financial risk in 1935 to virtually zero financial risk in 1936 (having been at enormous financial risk in 1891–95).

Table: summarised balance sheets of the Blackpool Tower Co.

Assets	1935	1936	Financing	1935	1936
	£	£		£	£
Property per cent Plant	662,473	643,039	Ordinary shares	412,500	412,500
Investment (W Gdns)	221,275	223,014	Preference shares	40,000	40,000
Stock per cent Debtors	18,140	18,420	Reserve fund	150,000	150,000
Cash	138,046	474	Maintenance fund	56,648	64,186
			Accumulated profit	112,727	126,894
			Equity – subtotal	771,875	793,580
			Tower debenture	120,000	-
			Palace debenture	100,000	-
			Creditors	48,059	61,671
			Overdraft	-	29,696
Totals	1,039,934	884,947	Totals	1,039,934	884,947

Source: drawn from published statements

This might be seen as prudent management, but finance theory would say that returns to shareholders are maximised by using debt. Debt attracts a fixed return in terms of interest, so if the company can make more than that on its activities, that adds to the wealth available to shareholders, even if it does increase the financial risk. In effect the board was making the Tower Co. less risky for shareholders, but also decreasing the rate of return.

Having too much cash is also a classical problem of a successful company that does not know how to continue to grow, or does not want to grow, or does not see opportunities to do so. An example in the twenty-first century would be the US company Apple, which is enormously successful, but seems unable to do anything with its cash: it had $160 billion in its balance sheet in the middle of 2014. Apple's case is complicated by international tax structures of course, but the problem is not a new one.

John Bickerstaffe generated value from the Tower but then used that to expand the Tower Co.'s base in Blackpool, buying successively, the Palace (Alhambra), the Grand Theatre, and as a final coup, the Winter Gardens Co. But after that the company expanded very little in Blackpool. From a strategic point of view, it was already by 1930 the dominant player in the Blackpool entertainment industry, and further expansion within the same sector would probably yield diminishing returns and emphasise the risk from lack of diversification.

A possible policy would have been to expand into the entertainment industry in a different location, using their industry knowledge but lessening the dependence on Blackpool. Buying theatres in Torquay for example, would have been smart, given the rise of that resort – but investment decisions are always easy in hindsight! The alternative would have been to buy in a different industry, but that has the risk of making mistakes through lack of experience of the sector. What the Tower Co. actually did during Robert Bickerstaffe's chairmanship was to keep its facilities up to date, pay down debt, and then finally just accumulate cash. This was invested in 'safe' securities and earned interest for the company.

The Opera House

The one major investment that the company did make was to rebuild and expand the Blackpool Opera House. The theatre had been designed by Matcham, and opened in 1889 within the Winter Gardens complex. Barry Band[5], in his history of the Opera House, says that it was the resort's first purpose-built theatre. It seated about 1800 people. In the 1930s the Tower management came to the conclusion that the theatre was not big enough for the expensive variety shows that were now being staged. They decided therefore to demolish the old theatre and build a new one.

In a significant feat of organisation, when the curtain went down on the 1938 summer season show on 16 October, building work started, and a modern 3,000 seat theatre opened its doors on 14 July 1939, with a review starring George Formby. The *Gazette* reported that the circle of the Opera House was supported by 'Blackpool's biggest ever girder'. This weighed 98 tons and arrived in sections by train at the end of December 1938. When assembled it was 114 feet long and eight-and-a-half feet high. To put the size of the new theatre in perspective, the Theatre Royal Drury Lane has a capacity of 2,220, the Palladium seats 2,300 and the Royal Opera House has a capacity of 2,256. Barry Band[6] says that the whole development cost £125,000 – not inconsiderable by comparison with the Winter Gardens share capital of £105,000.

Once again, the timing was unfortunate. 1938 had been marked by major diplomatic tensions in Europe, as Germany sought to expand its borders. The tension subsided somewhat with Chamberlain's compromise with Hitler, but in 1939 tension built up again and holidaymakers stayed away from Blackpool, giving the Tower Co. one of its worst ever seasons.

A footnote to the pre-war period is that in 1937 a certain Barnet Winogradsky presented his exotic dance act at the Palace, appearing, according to Barry Band[7], with Toko his oriental dance partner, in a variety show. This was the start of a long association that was to be very significant for the Tower Co. decades later. Mr Winogradsky, brother of Lew and Leslie Grade, after the Second World War came to dominate show business in Blackpool, under his stage name, Bernard Delfont, ultimately seeing the Tower Co. bought into EMI's leisure division, which he then chaired.

9

THE SECOND WORLD WAR

People were much better prepared for the Second World War than the first. Hitler and his National Socialist Party had come to power in the early 1930s and the political tension had been growing over several years. The 1938 annexation of Austria and the invasion of Czechoslovakia had raised all sorts of concerns that war was definitely coming, with people being issued with gas masks and digging shelters. In the end the war did not come until a year later, but the planning had continued, and, as Turner and Palmer[1] report, trains full of evacuated children started to turn up in Blackpool on 3 September 1939, the day the British ultimatum expired. Civil servants started to relocate to Blackpool at the same time.

The evacuees would go home again in 1940, but the civil service stayed and took over more and more hotels and other accommodation. The experience of the First World War had been noted, and Blackpool's extensive accommodation, large public buildings and open spaces were ideal for training. The Royal Air Force took over the Winter Gardens during the daytime for training purposes, and billeted its trainees all over Blackpool. The top of the Tower became a radar installation. A factory to build Wellington bombers opened and the US Air Force established an air base near Lytham, seven miles to the south. Although Blackpool's holidaymakers had temporarily disappeared (and returned later), they were replaced with a year-round demand not only for accommodation, but for entertainment, food and drink.

For the Blackpool Tower Co. there was good news and bad. The good news was the year-round season; it fed the asset utilisation nirvana of being able to have buildings used all day that previously were used only in the evenings. The RAF showed training films in the Opera House during the day and used the Empress Ballroom as a gym, while the buildings reverted to entertainment in the evening.

The bad news was hugely increased taxation. The experience of the First World War had been taken on board by the government in this area as well, and it moved quickly to impose an Excess Profits Tax to soak up profits generated by war activity, and it quickly ramped up the rates of income tax and entertainments tax.

A side effect was the introduction of the Pay As You Earn (PAYE) income tax deduction system which enormously complicated the administration of wages from April 1944. The tax system was extended to bring in to its net many relatively low-paid staff who had not previously paid tax. The PAYE system was introduced to enable them to pay week by week instead of in two large instalments in a year which was the standard method. During the year the Tower Co. had approximately 1,000 staff when operating fully.

Taxation

The Entertainments Tax had been introduced in 1916 as part of the First World War financing, as discussed in Chapter Six, but had never been repealed, despite vociferous complaints from the industry, especially the cinemas. All the government needed to do was to increase the rates. The impact on the Tower Co. is shown in the table.

Table 9.1: Entertainments Tax paid by Blackpool Tower Co.

	Year	£
	1939	39,394
	1940	36,852
Rate increase	1941	78,709
Rate increase	1942	136,796
Rate increase	1943	208,333

Year	£
1944	229,655
1945	260,496
1946	294,090
1947	229,428
Rate reduction 1948	165,154

Source: Tower Co. yearbooks

The government had introduced a 5 per cent tax on company profits in 1937 which was called the National Defence Contribution. It then went on to introduce an Excess Profits Tax in 1939 at a rate of 60 per cent on profits above a pre-war average. This rose to 100 per cent as from 1 April 1940 and remained at that level until 1 January 1946 when it dropped to 60 per cent before being repealed at the end of that year.

Hicks et al[2] point out that Excess Profits Tax (EPT) was 'in direct line of succession' from the Excess Profits Duty (EPD) of the First World War. They add that it was clear that EPT was intended to be 'a more drastic tax' than EPD and the legislation made sure that were far fewer grounds for appeals and concessions in its application. As with EPD, the 'excess' was calculated in relation to a pre-war year, but with EPT this had to be either 1935 or 1936, or the average of either year with 1937. As it happens this was advantageous for the Tower Co. for whom 1935, 1936 and 1937 were all particularly profitable years (see Chapter Eight).

Hicks et al say they were surprised at the early increase in the rate of EPT to 100 per cent, a rate not charged during the First World War. They explain that the rationale was that on the one hand, as much money as possible was needed to pay for the war, and on the other hand, the government wished to be able to control the economy. If companies benefiting from war profits were able to invest the excess profits or pay it to shareholders as dividends, this would unleash demand for assets which would compete with the needs of the war economy to produce munitions.

The authors note that companies had also to pay income tax, and despite the government's efforts, the rate of inflation increased so the 'excess' profits included the effects of inflation on the pre-war average profits. The consequence was that companies in effect had their disposable profits restricted to below the pre-war average.

Daunton[3] explains that in the First World War politicians had expected to pay for the war primarily by borrowing and only secondarily by increased taxation. However this had been blamed for inflation, and in the approach to the Second World War, they intended to reverse this by radically increasing taxation and funding the war primarily from that revenue.

As regards income tax, the threshold at which people became liable to pay tax was lowered and the rates increased. This meant that weekly-paid workers now fell into the tax net, and generated the need to provide a deduction from the pay packet, because people at that time expected to be able to spend everything they took home. This eventually motivated the government to invent PAYE so that employers collected the tax on a weekly basis.

Daunton describes the situation (p177) as being one of a 'period of phoney taxation' as well as a 'phoney war' in the first few months following the declaration of war. After that EPT went up to 100 per cent although there was opposition to it. J. M. Keynes was one of several economists appointed to the Economics Section of the cabinet office, and as Daunton said: 'he was now an insider and could not simply be ignored'. Keynes considered that the Excess Profits Tax was ill-conceived because it provided a solid disincentive to companies to increase production, even though the government might well need them to expand production to help the war effort or substitute for imports. It was also potentially biased by the fact that, just before the war, companies were still recovering from the severe depression of the 1930s and were earning below normal profits anyway so their pre-war base line for excess profits was artificially low.

The government, however, had the same concern as in the First World War that there should be no profiteering as a result of the war. They eventually decided to retain the 100 per cent rate (on profits above the pre-war average) but to refund 20 per cent once the war was over. A side effect of this was that the reported profits became very difficult to interpret because tax that was charged 1939–46 would to some extent flow back into profit over the following years.

Coincidentally the war period was also one where there was a lot of discussion of financial reporting by listed companies. A government commission (Cohen Commission) was set up and reported in 1945, proposing many changes which through the 1947 Companies Act set out a lot of the ground rules that still affect reporting. During this period the way in which the Tower Co. presented its profit or loss statement and balance sheet changed several times, possibly reflecting the changing nature of best practice. Up until 1942 the company gave no separate information about tax at all, either in the profit or loss, or balance sheet. From 1942 it started to report tax outstanding at the balance sheet date. In 1947 it started to show a tax charge in profit or loss: it revealed a charge of £113,116 for 1947, and, another innovation, it started publishing comparative figures for the previous year, which included divulging a 1946 tax charge of £210,874.

Table 9.2: Reported earnings, depreciation and taxation

Year	Earnings	Depreciation	Tax owed
	£	£	£
1939	28,825	-	
1940	43,207	25,000	
1941	52,801	25,000	
1942	60,609	30,000	230,261
1943	59,590	30,000	244,159
1944	60,146	30,000	320,982
1945	67,837	30,000	282,887
1946	97,321	30,000	297,890
1947	154,374	30,000	274,071

Source: published financial statements

The figures (table 9.2) show that the published earnings number remained approximately at the level of the 1920s and only in 1947 did it get back to a six figure sum comparable to the mid-1930s. However, this is not to be taken quite at face value. The company used the annual depreciation as a variable charge. It had not charged depreciation between 1921 and 1934, and had then charged variable amounts from 1935 to 1938. There was no depreciation in the very poor 1939 performance, but then a charge for £25,000 was made in 1940. To compare 1939 with 1940, this should be added back, to get a 1940 profit of £68,207 and 1945 £97,837 on a comparable basis.

This was nothing unusual at the time, and was perfectly transparent in that any shareholder could see the figures in the published financial statements, even if today it would be regarded as profit management. Certainly the board did not want to be seen to be making excess profits from the war, and equally, the company was paying very substantial taxes. On the basis of the limited information available, it looks as if the Tower Co. was paying at least £200,000 a year in Entertainments Tax and another £200,000 in various income taxes. So if the shareholders were not seeing boom profits, the company was making a big financial contribution to the government.

Companies were indeed very severely taxed. They paid income tax at 10s in the pound (i.e. 50 per cent). They also paid the National Defence Contribution of 5 per cent, and 100 per cent tax on profits in excess of the pre-war average. On top of that the government introduced a special company tax which was higher on profit distributed as a dividend – the aim being to encourage companies to retain cash and not to pay dividends.

Another aspect of government taxation policy was the aim of dampening down consumer demand. In the earlier war, wages had risen and triggered inflationary increases in demand. The government decided in 1942 to increase tax on 'optional expenditure' on items such as beer, tobacco and entertainment (Daunton p185) to peg back demand.

The Entertainment Business

A particular feature of theatres in particular, but also of cinemas and ballrooms, is that most of the costs of running them are 'fixed' in accounting terminology. That means that within a particular trading period they have to be absorbed whether or not there are any customers. The theatre has to be heated, it has to be maintained, it has to have stage, box office and other staff and it has to advertise, irrespective of whether there is one customer or 2,000. The same is true for the show producer, who has to supply scenery and costumes and pay the cast whether anyone watches or not. The Ballroom has the same building and staff costs plus the cost of a band. The cinema is slightly different in that the theatre owner normally pays a percentage of receipts to the film distributor, so that a significant cost is 'variable' – moves up and down according to the level of business.

The relevance of this is that each year the entertainments companies are in effect making a bet, when they sign contracts to engage artists for the whole of the next season, that there will be enough visitors and the show will attract enough of them to meet the fixed costs, and ideally enough to make big profits after that. However, if something happens, as happened in 1939, that the season is in effect brought to an end two months before that was expected, the entertainment companies are left having to pay all their acts and staff with virtually no revenue coming in. This happened in 1914 and to a greater extent in 1939.

In the Second World War people would have been more aware of the risk of war, as a result of the events in the preceding years, and were probably reluctant to travel and possibly wanting to conserve savings. The 1939 season was a disaster. The war was confirmed on 3 September, and immediately plans to evacuate children and to relocate key activities out of London meant that the railways were under pressure.

In Blackpool the illuminations in October were cancelled, not least on the grounds of the blackout. In fact the government imposed an absolute blackout from 1 September. In the run up to war planners had taken the view that Britain would be subject to night bombing raids, and had decided on the blackout as a necessary counter-measure. Leaflets were issued earlier in the year to explain what was needed, and the blackout was imposed before the war had even formally begun.

There was no question therefore of the illuminations being allowed, but from a business perspective the illuminations served the purpose of extending the season until the end of October. Entertainments and all the other related services were contracted and had to be paid even though there were no visitors. Barry Band reports that the show at the Opera House ran until 7 October. For the Tower Co. net earnings in 1939 were £28,825, compared with £96,002 in 1938 and £128,402 in 1937. Visitor numbers had been down already in 1938, as a result of the political crisis in Europe, but this was as nothing compared to 1939, when the season in effect ended two months early.

However, if the 1939 season was a disaster, thereafter as Walton[4] remarks:

> Blackpool did at least as well out of the Second World War as the first one, and its role as a military training centre introduced its delights to a further array of newcomers, some of whom returned as honeymooners in the post-war marriage boom.' He added (p137) 'Blackpool gained more than it lost by wartime conditions between 1939 and 1945, especially as many of its competitors on the east and south coasts were incapacitated for the duration by military occupation and the threats of invasion and aerial bombardment.

He notes that more than 750,000 RAF recruits passed through the town, with as many as 45,000 resident at a peak time. This created employment and, given the shortage of staff, led to a significant increase in wages. He says that the aircraft factory at Squire's Gate employed 10,000 people at its peak and by the end of the war there were more than 15,000 civil servants based in the area. On top of the year-round employment created by the war, there were still significant if shorter summer seasons, given the closure of many resort areas, with many holiday visitors, despite the war.

The Opera House, which had been enlarged and rebuilt for the 1939 season, looked as if it were going to hit difficulties since it did not open until the middle of July. Then the government decreed that theatres should close when war was declared at the beginning of September. Barry Band[5] reports that this ban was lifted in a matter of days, and the show went on. However, there was a shortage of touring shows big enough to fill the Opera House, and it operated as a cinema in the autumn. In the major rebuilding the Tower Co. had provided a modern projection room to enable the theatre to operate as a cinema. This had the advantage, not envisaged in the planning stage, that the RAF could use it to show training films during the daytime.

He also says another unintended consequence was that once the blitz started in London towards the end of 1940 Jack Hylton and George Black, major impresarios of the time, shifted their show-producing offices to Blackpool. This was part of a major shift of attention by the theatrical world, given that Blackpool theatres continued to function throughout the war. Aside from variety stars such as George Formby, and singers Anne Ziegler and Webster Booth, Band cites Vivien Leigh (star of Gone with the Wind) appearing in a Shaw play at the Grand Theatre, and doing a charity Sunday concert at the Opera House with husband Laurence Olivier. John Gielgud appeared at the Opera House in his production of *Macbeth* in 1942. Malcolm Sargent conducted the Bournemouth Symphony Orchestra in concert at the Opera House.

The Palace was very busy, being used for training and related activities in the day and reverting to a variety theatre by night. In June 1940 it featured a presentation by a very young double act, Eric Morecambe and Ernie Wise. Its mainstream attractions included Vera Lynn and Stephane Grappelli, the latter a refugee from German-occupied Paris.

It can be seen that the war had a tremendous – and beneficial – effect on Blackpool, which enjoyed an economic boom. However, the impact of that boom was not really felt by the Tower Co., to the extent that swingeing additional taxes were sucking all the profit from the business, which was probably contributing more than £400,000 a year to the government through income tax, National Defence Contribution, company tax, Excess Profits Tax and Entertainments Tax. The company was also left with the problems of bringing its activities back to peacetime operation from 1946, and catching up with all the repairs and maintenance that had been deferred during the war, and were still difficult to do in the shortage of materials as the government tried to direct the post-war economy.

THE LAST OF THE BICKERSTAFFES

Views differ about when the UK resort industry started to decline significantly. Some point to the development of Devon and Cornwall as resort destinations after 1945, aided by the growth in car ownership, as drawing some of the demand away from the traditional resorts. This was followed by the advent of television, which changed people's leisure habits, and eventually the package holiday to the Mediterranean, which at first only attracted middle-class holidaymakers, but by the 1970s was taken up much more widely.

John Walton[1] notes that while Blackpool visitor numbers held up into the 1970s, the length of time which people stayed was going down, and the town was attracting fewer teenagers. He suggests that the practice of taking family holidays was disappearing. He observes that the 'crowded beaches and inclusive family parties of the 1960s are close to the end of an era'. He adds that the prosperity of the 1960s 'masked a failure to recruit enough of the new generation ... and a change in the social profile of the visitors, which if left unchecked might have generated a subsequent collapse of the holiday industry on the pattern which soon became widespread elsewhere.'(p145)

As regards the entertainment business, Barry Band[2] refers to the decade after the Second World War as the golden period of variety in Blackpool, but says that from 1955 the business started to move off its peak, with television becoming an important competitor. Many live theatres around the country closed in the late 1950s and 1960s, including the major touring theatre circuits.

He also points out that ballroom dancing started to be displaced by rock'n'roll and later discotheques.

Whatever the future held, in 1945 Blackpool quickly moved back to a prosperous peace-time mode, which it was to enjoy for at least another fifteen years, before starting to feel the onslaught of television and foreign holidays. Coincidentally, this was also roughly the period when the Tower Company was chaired by the last of the Bickerstaffes. Douglas Bickerstaffe became chairman at the end of 1947, when his cousin Robert Bickerstaffe stood down from the board (and died within a year).

Unlike his cousin, Douglas Bickerstaffe lived in Blackpool and took a detailed interest in the running of the company. While Robert Bickerstaffe had kept the ship on course through the Second World War, he had not attempted to expand its activities. As discussed in Chapter Eight, he had made profits, accumulated cash and paid off debt. He did not attempt to expand in Blackpool or elsewhere, nor, for that matter, did he return cash to shareholders, as would have been expected by the markets now. A large part of the Tower Co.'s balance sheet consisted of financial assets when Douglas took over:

Table 10.1 Financial assets in consolidated balance sheet
BTC Financial assets 1948–1967

Year	Total	Government securities	Cash	Tax certificates	Quoted securities
	£	£	£	£	£
1948	1,153,561	442,395	511,166	200,000	
1949	1,304,397	442,395	827,027	34,975	
1950	1,200,666	442,395	518,271	240,000	
1951	1,170,156	448,424	481,732	240,000	
1952	1,149,202	452,714	406,488	290,000	
1953	1,147,252	427,214	465,038	255,000	
1954	1,198,872	337,714	611,158	250,000	
1955	1,124,376	422,716	451,660	250,000	

BTC Financial assets 1948–1967

Year	Total	Government securities	Cash	Tax certificates	Quoted securities
1956	1,123,697	372,716	475,981	275,000	
1957	1,064,199	374,675	391,663	260,575	47,286
1958	950,090	453,220	230,219	231,500	35,151
1959	685,567	287,714	154,014	160,050	83,789
1960	879,873	287,714	382,720	125,650	83,789
1961	681,118	287,714	269,258	91,544	32,602
1962	585,005	287,714	264,689	-	32,602
1963	415,326	138,334	244,390	-	32,602
1964	393,094	138,334	244,996	-	9,764
1965	242,650	108,335	124,551	-	9,764
1966	210,496	67,075	143,421	-	-
1967	145,521	69,832	75,689	-	-

Source: published financial statements

When Douglas became chairman, the balance sheet contained more than a million pounds of financial assets, constituting more than half the group's total assets of £1.9 million: quite astonishing for a seaside resort company. Douglas Bickerstaffe did indeed try to expand, but his efforts went more into the area of property development, and he bought a car dealership, making the Tower Co. a very strange mini-conglomerate – and largely getting rid of Robert's treasure chest in the late 1950s and early 1960s. When he resigned from the board in 1964 (he had stood down from the chair in 1961), the company was soon snapped up by EMI, then a major international conglomerate with interests ranging between records (both classical and popular), defence electronics, television (it made studio equipment, but also later owned the Thames Television Co., which had the weekday franchise for London), and show business.

Financial Performance

Robert Bickerstaffe's stewardship of the company during the Second World War had largely mirrored that of his father during the First World War. The business had switched to year-round operations, had paid significant taxes to the government, but had also helped the war effort by investing its surplus cash in government securities. He had bought tax certificates as well, an investment rarely seen today, but then a conservative gesture which involved in effect paying your taxes in advance, receiving a (usually low) rate of interest on them, and then cashing them in when it was time to settle the tax bill. Holding large cash balances is also a rather conservative management strategy, suggesting a lack of appetite for risk. Unlike his father, Robert did not sell off his government holdings after the war.

It should be borne in mind, however, that the government's taxation and economic policies were directed towards encouraging companies not to pay money to shareholders by way of big dividends. According to Daunton[3] the 1945 Labour government was faced with two conflicting policy objectives: it wanted to redistribute wealth, and it also wanted to rebuild Britain's position as a major international trading nation.

One way it tried to achieve this was by taxing dividends heavily, to give companies an incentive to retain cash and use it for investment in capacity and renovation. It also tried to restrict domestic demand so that production was available for export. Daunton says that economic historians think this policy was not effective and in fact led to post war stagnation and lack of innovation. In any event, its effect on the Tower Co. was to encourage the build-up of financial resources, without investing in new activities.

In fact it took the country a long time to work its way out of war and return to normal peacetime activities. Sweet rationing was still in force in the 1950s. Bill Curtis[4] notes, however, that the lifts in the Tower came back into service in 1946 and Reginald

Dixon returned from military service to play the Wurlitzer once more. She adds, though, that 'almost all the necessary materials were in short supply and so progress was slow.' The Blackpool illuminations did not start again until 1949. John Walton[5] comments, however, that Blackpool recovered from the war much more quickly than resorts on the south coast whose beaches had been shut off and sometimes mined, and whose boarding houses had gone out of business. Turner and Palmer[6] say that Blackpool enjoyed a boom of visitors after the war and claim that the early post-war period brought huge profits to the entertainment business.

Nonetheless, as in the First World War, little had been done in terms of repairs and maintenance and it took some years to get the resort back into physical shape. Barry Band[7] quotes Bernard Crabtree (a senior Tower manager – see Chapter Seven) as saying that the Palace was refurbished only at the start of 1950. 'The shortage of paints and materials in the austere years after the war had delayed the job but the work crews moved in on January 9, 1950. It hadn't been done since 1919 and it was in a shabby state.' Bill Curtis[8] says that it was 1952 before 'the whole town had been restored to peacetime appearance'.

Table 10.2 Extracts from consolidated profit and loss account
BTC Consolidated after tax profits

Year to 31 October	£ Reported Profit	£ Provision created	£ Repairs charged	£ Adjusted profit
1948	248,998			248,998
1949	224,311			224,311
1950	171,459		-36,720	134,739
1951*	108,916	52,518	-	161,434
1952	151,826	45,000	-52294	144,532
1953	148,605	40,000	-38,404	150,201

BTC Consolidated after tax profits

Year to 31 October	£	£	£	£
	Reported Profit	Provision created	Repairs charged	Adjusted profit
1954	150,020	36,901	-38,881	148,040
1955	145,677	50,000	-75,992	119,685
1956	125,849	75,000	-74,592	125,897
1957	144,879	75,000	-35,037	184,842
1958	87,479	50,000	-55,339	82,140
1959	128,052	50,000	-49,873	128,179
1960	137,964	50,000	-61,483	126,481
1961	157,811	50,000	-44,207	163,604
1962	140,044	40,000	-38,247	141,797
1963	136,347	40,000	-46,662	129,685
1964	176,036	45,000	-41,414	179,622
1965	227,378	55,000	-54,652	227,726
1966	216,544	40,000	-39,565	216,979
1967	145,214	22,500	-22,425	145,289

*1951 figures are estimates based on 1950 and 1952 statements
Source: published financial statements

The separate financial performance of the Blackpool Tower Company's entertainment activities became more difficult to analyse from 1948 as a result of the 1947 Companies Act. This was a major landmark in British financial reporting which introduced a large number of reforms. One of the most fundamental was the requirement to produce 'consolidated' financial statements. The idea was that linked companies that form a group run by the same ultimate management, such as the Tower Co. and the Winter Gardens Co., must produce financial statements as though they were a single company.

The reason for this is that it is easy to mislead if there is a group of related companies but the investor only sees a subset of these. Famous financial scandals have occurred through one side of a set of transactions being invisible to the investor.[9] But quite apart from that, there are lots of internal allocations done when accounting for related companies – for example, if, as would be normal, they share the same accounts department, company secretary and auditor, how are the costs split between the companies? That problem disappears in consolidated accounts where internal transactions are cancelled, and the whole is treated as a single legal entity, even if in fact it comprises hundreds of companies in different countries (e.g. an international group like Nestlé).

So from 1948 onwards the profits from both the Tower Co. and the Winter Gardens Co. were rolled together, and the group figures are not strictly comparable with the earlier figures which showed the Tower Co. including a dividend from the Winter Gardens but not the whole Winter Gardens result. From 1959 onwards the figures also include earnings from the non-entertainment activities undertaken by the group.

A further complication is that from either 1951 or 1952 (the 1951 financial statements were not available) the company started a curious practice of charging a provision for repairs against profits, and then offsetting the actual costs against the provision. Nowadays regulators are a lot more sceptical about the use of provisions, but the principle is that a company knows it has an expense coming up, and charges an estimate against the current profits, rather than letting the actual expenses flow into the next year's accounts.

The rationale that could be advanced in the Tower Group's case is that it was necessary to make good in the low season the wear and tear of the high season just finished, and that logically the cost of the making good should be charged against the profits of the high season just gone, not the next one. That fits with the fundamental principle that accounts report sales of the time period, but charge against those sales all the costs incurred to make the sales, irrespective of when those costs are settled. This is known as the 'matching' principle.

However, provisions could also be used to manage profits from one year to another, and to 'smooth' them – hence the suspicion with which they are now treated. Table 10.2 shows the reported net profit after tax, but then adds back the provision and deducts the actual expenditure, to get to an unmanaged profit. You can see that the effect was sometimes to move profits between years, but there is nothing too exaggerated, and the pattern of reported profits is not significantly different to that of the adjusted profit in the right hand column.

The table demonstrates that the Tower Group reached a peak in the late 1940s that it would not achieve again until the mid-1960s, by which time inflation would have reduced the value of the pound significantly. The profit included property development and garage activities as well as the entertainment activities and the Palace had become a department store.

Expansion and Diversification

Bill Curtis[10] says that Douglas Bickerstaffe had gone to school in Blackpool, but had subsequently been sent to Heidelberg, where he was interned during the First World War. As an adult he had worked for the American Express Co. in Germany. The *Gazette*, in his obituary in 1965, specified that he had gone to the Arnold School in Blackpool and then the Heidelberg College. While the name Heidelberg probably conjures up the picture of the historic town and its university, one of the oldest in the world, Douglas Bickerstaffe was born in 1895, the younger son of Tom Bickerstaffe, and according to the *Gazette* started work for American Express in Berlin from 1911, when he would have been sixteen years old, so the Heidelberg College referred to must have been some institution for secondary education. He was still in Germany in 1914 and was interned.

Both his schooling in Germany and his internment are mentioned in the newspapers, but no more than that. It seems extraordinary that a youngster from Blackpool should be sent to Germany for schooling, and also that he should not have returned at the outbreak of war and been called up for military service. However, his early life gets only the briefest mention in articles in the local newspapers, despite its very unusual nature.

Douglas returned to Blackpool to look after his father's fleet of paddle steamers at the end of the War. The *Gazette* says he joined the Blackpool Passenger Steamboat Co. in 1918. However, the popularity of the steamers was waning, and when the company ceased trading in 1923, Douglas bought the steamer *Bickerstaffe* (commissioned originally by his uncle and grandfather) and ran it from the North Pier until 1928. He was also a principal in an attraction called Fairyland on the central promenade, which Barry Band described as 'turning garden gnomes into an amusement'. In 1934 he succeeded his father as a director of the Clifton Hotel, and replaced his father on the Tower Co. board in 1937. He was appointed a Justice of the Peace in 1953.

He took over as chairman of the Tower Co. in 1947, when his cousin Robert retired through ill health. Robert had lived in Liverpool and presumably limited his activities to conducting board meetings and participating in official functions. Douglas, on the other hand, lived in Blackpool and took a close interest in the day to day operations of the company. Bill Curtis[11] says that 'Rarely a day passed without Douglas making an appearance in the Tower, smoking Woodbine cigarettes with the ash dropping down his waistcoat.'

The immediate challenge when Douglas became chairman was to get the Company's premises back to the high state of repair that had always been a hallmark. As discussed earlier, this was difficult in the light of the absence of materials and the government's attempts to direct resources to manufacturing.

However, by 1950 the company's assets were largely in shape, and Douglas could turn to questions of expansion.

He had the opportunity to buy a competitor variety theatre known as Feldman's in 1951, and failed to do so. As related in Barry Band's account of the Palace[12], Feldman's was a large theatre staging variety shows and was located in Bank Hey Street just up from the Tower and the Palace. It was regarded as the second variety venue after the Palace. Feldman, the owner, died in 1949 and eventually the theatre was put up for auction.

Under John Bickerstaffe this would have been seen as an opportunity to eliminate a competitor, and prevent giving a toehold in Blackpool to any of the larger outside entertainment companies. Douglas Bickerstaffe saw it in much the same way, but the auction was held in London, and, according to Band, who quotes Crabtree, a member of the Tower management, he contented himself with instructing an agent to bid up to £70,000. His intention was to buy the property and close it down as a theatre, leaving the Palace free of competition for both performers and audience.

However, he had reckoned without an Irishman, James Brennan, evidently an outsider in terms of Blackpool's business establishment. He was reputed to have made his fortune from dealing in scrap metal after the First World War, and subsequently established himself in St Anne's. He went on to build up a small chain of entertainment venues around Lancashire. Band quotes Crabtree as saying that the Tower Co. had bid on the property value as they considered Feldman's to be too run down to be of interest to anyone as a theatre, even though it had 1,680 seats and three licensed bars and was being offered as a going concern. The Tower agent stopped bidding at £70,000, and Brennan walked away with the theatre for £71,500 in June 1952.

The Ballroom Fire

At the end of 1956 the Tower suffered another fire. The *Financial Times* of 15 December reported that the fire had 'raged for six hours' but that it was fully covered by insurance and the Company expected the Tower to be back in full service in time for the following season. Bill Curtis reports that the fire spread under the floor of the ballroom and caused significant damage – such that the ballroom was out of service for the whole of 1957 and the Company reopened the ballroom in the Palace as a substitute. The subsequent annual reports reveal that the Tower Co. had 'loss of profits' insurance for the Ballroom, which would normally have covered the absence of profit, but such policies typically require the insured to do as much as possible to mitigate the losses incurred, which would have encouraged them to reopen the Palace. In fact negotiations on the insurance claim were still going on as late as 1960.

One of the reasons for the long reconstruction period was that Douglas Bickerstaffe decided that the Tower Ballroom should be fully restored to its previous condition, as designed by Frank Matcham. Nowadays the Tower Ballroom is regarded as an architectural gem and a national treasure – for example dancing there is one of the official high points of the BBC programme *Strictly Come Dancing*. However, at the time it must have been a very difficult decision. Television had arrived. Certainly it was still relatively rudimentary in the mid-1950s, but it must have been clear that it was bound to have a major impact on people's leisure habits.

Some managements might have asked themselves whether it was worth reestablishing the ballroom, or, if doing so, going to the vast expense of recreating the expensive plasterwork and murals. At the time, people were typically keener to demolish and modernise their town centres rather than to preserve. Bernard Crabtree wrote[13] 'Literally hundreds of letters arrived, asking for the ballroom to be restored'. Bill Curtis[14] reports that 'despite pressure to modernise the ballroom (Douglas Bickerstaffe) was firm in his decision that it should be restored as Frank Matcham had designed it'. Nonetheless, the Tower lounge, which had also been destroyed, was not returned to its nineteenth century splendour but replaced with a modern café.

The Tower Ballroom reopened in May 1958. Vanessa Toulmin[15] says that Bickerstaffe issued a public invitation to everyone who had attended the original opening in 1894 to come to the reopening. Turner & Palmer[16] comment: 'In retrospect the reopening of the Ballroom was something of a watershed in the development of Blackpool's entertainments for soon afterwards the familiar pattern of the industry began to change.' The most obvious and dramatic example was the demolition of the Palace and the construction on the site of a department store, and indeed the closure of the Palace could be seen as a more obvious indicator of a sea change than the reconstruction of the Tower Ballroom.

The Start of the Decline

Turner and Palmer say that the post-war years were 'the golden years for entertainment in Blackpool with its 15 cinemas and 14 live shows, offering the best-known names in show business'.

Bernard Crabtree[17], however, commented that 'Variety survived the coming of radio and talking pictures but was killed off by the growing popularity of television, particularly the arrival of commercial television in 1956'. He explained it as a 'two fold slump' – the audience stayed at home to watch the live shows on television, and the artists themselves wanted to work on television and avoid the gruelling travel involved in performing all over the country.

Barry Band also cites Bernard Crabtree as saying that variety was in decline from about then. He said: 'From early 1955 we found it difficult to assemble decent variety bills for the Palace.' The Palace had staged some variety shows in the off season as well as the summer, but these stopped in 1957. The Palace featured summer variety shows from Bernard Delfont in 1960 and 1961, and then closed its doors for the last time.

Although the official announcement of its closure was not made until the start of the 1961 season, this must have been in Douglas Bickerstaffe's mind for some time. In October 1959 the Tower Co. made an offer worth about £180,000 for the shares of County Hotel (Blackpool) Ltd, an offer recommended by County's board of directors. On 26 October 1959 the brokers acting for the Tower Co. reported that 94 per cent of the ordinary shares had been sold to them, and the bid became unconditional (the rest of the shares were acquired in 1960).

Why did the Tower Co. want the County Hotel? Was it about to expand into the hotel business? That would have been a logical development, albeit one that would emphasise the company's exposure to the vagaries of the Blackpool holiday season, but no, the County Hotel occupied part of an island site in the Blackpool town plan, the rest of which was occupied by the Palace. In the annual report for the year to 31 October 1959, Douglas Bickerstaffe wrote: 'To further the future development of the company, your directors have considered it advisable to control the whole of the Island Site on the Blackpool Promenade, which includes the Palace buildings and the County Hotel.'

No redevelopment plan was announced at this time, but shortly afterwards Billy Smart (one of the leading circus operators at that time) put in a bid to buy the Palace from the Tower Co. The *Financial Times* of 6 January 1960 quotes Smart's son David as saying that the offer was in the region of £1 million. Bickerstaffe rejected the offer, commenting that the board was still considering the best way of developing the Palace. The *Daily Express* quotes Bickerstaffe as dismissing Billy Smart's offer as 'nothing more than evidence of the general interest in this matter'.

During 1960 Bickerstaffe commissioned a valuation of the group's properties. In a note to the 1960 financial statements, the company reported that the group properties had been valued at

£3,728,100, specifying that the Palace/County Hotel had been valued for its development, but the rest of the property in its current use. The book value of the properties was £803,376. A disparity was to be expected in that the property was recorded in the books at its historical cost, so much of the physical asset base was at prices ruling in the 1890s when the Tower was built.

The next information to be published was not until the beginning of the 1961 season, when the Tower Co. announced the planned closure of the Palace Theatre, and their intention to demolish the Palace and the County Hotel, and build a department store in partnership with Lewis's[18] (not to be confused with the John Lewis Partnership). In their six monthly report (an innovation) they said they were considering a partnership with a property developer, the Hammerson Group, to develop their property interests. But the Palace site would involve them in financing £500,000 of construction. They were considering forming a separate company to administer their property interests – and by the way, they had acquired a controlling interest (actually 60 per cent) of Brown and Mallalieu, a large car dealer.

Barry Band points out[19] that news of the demolition of the Palace was portrayed the *Blackpool Gazette* as good for the resort. He adds that Sir Harold Grime, the then editor of the *Gazette*, was also deputy chairman of the Tower Co.

The Last Bickerstaffe

In May 1961 Douglas Bickerstaffe resigned as chairman of the company, while remaining a director. He is quoted as having said that it was time for a younger man to take over. Barry Band[20] says that Bickerstaffe who 'was not a well man, and was prone to drinking one too many' gave an interview to a *Daily Mirror* journalist in which he speculated on the future of the company, and the possibility it might have to be sold. The editor of the *Blackpool Gazette*, Harold Grime, played the story down, according to Band, but directors of Mecca, which itself was originally a ballroom company, came to Blackpool to discuss a takeover[21]. The Tower board were horrified, and rejected the approach out of hand, but then pressured Bickerstaffe into resigning as chairman.

It is easy to see the demolition of the Palace as a critical turning point for the company. For the first time since John Bickerstaffe had taken the chair in 1891, the company was reducing its entertainment footprint not increasing it. Equally the Palace had been one of John Bickerstaffe's more spectacular coups, taking it out of bankruptcy at a knock-down price and making it very profitable, so there is a whiff of failing to preserve the empire he had created. There was a certain dramatic completeness about announcing the destruction of the Palace and resigning at the same time, becoming the last Bickerstaffe to serve as chairman, after the family had run the Tower Co. continuously for seventy years.

Douglas remained on the board, but resigned three years later, and died in 1965, two years before the company was taken over by EMI at the instigation of Bernard Delfont. The *Gazette* (24 August 1965) noted that he had been ill for a long time and confined to his bed. The priest at his funeral said he was 'a man of great simplicity who liked the ordinary straightforward things of life. He was known to all people for his extraordinary love of Blackpool ... he was a very shy man, very reserved, but if you got behind the shyness and the reserve, you found he was always very kind.' He added: 'His thought was entertainment of the family. Nothing that was sordid or mean should be put before a family.'

The New Chairman

The board appointed Dr George Edward ('Ted') Badman as chairman. Badman had been a director since 1949, and like Bickerstaffe was the current representative of a Blackpool family which had a long-standing major share stake in the Tower Co. The Badmans had in fact been significant shareholders in the

Winter Gardens Co. and had acquired their Tower Co. stake in the takeover of the Winter Gardens by the Tower. Frederick Badman had been on the board of the Winter Gardens since the 1890s (Band[22]) but when he died, in 1924, and his shares passed to his son, Charles Badman, the son was not offered a seat on the board. He took the rejection badly, and joined with the widowed Mrs Huddlestone, equally rejected by the Winter Gardens board, in proposing the takeover by the Tower Co. He was appointed a director of the Winter Gardens Co. after the takeover and later joined the board of the Tower Co.

Ted Badman had joined the Tower board when his father died. The *Gazette* reported that he was forty-five years of age when he became chairman, and had previously been chairman of the finance committee of the company. He was a medical practitioner and a local directory for 1952/53 records him as having a practice in Blackpool. A British Medical Association directory for 1962/63 lists him as based then in Cleveleys (a somewhat upmarket town near Blackpool). Barry Band says he was an anaesthetist at Blackpool Victoria Hospital.[23] He lived until 1997.

The 1961 financial statements suggest that one of the first things the new chairman did was to pay about £95,000 for the 60 per cent shareholding in the car dealership, which had showrooms in the centre of Blackpool next to the Winter Gardens, and sold BMC vehicles.[24] In the chairman's report, the company said that Brown and Mallalieu had contributed £23,000 to group profits for 1961 for the five months it had been a subsidiary. The chairman's report also drew attention to conference business as being a growing source of profit. He pointed out that due to the availability of facilities capable of holding a large audience, and of plentiful accommodation, the town was becoming more popular as a conference venue.

In January 1962 the *Financial Times* reported that the Tower Co. was to develop the Palace/County Hotel site by constructing a building at a cost of £2.5 million in conjunction with Lewis's. The Tower would contribute £0.5 million for which it would own a series of individual shops within the overall development, comprising 45,000 square feet at basement, ground floor and first floor level. Lewis's would occupy the rest of the 225,000 square feet of the six-storey building. The article said that construction was scheduled to be finished by the end of 1963, with the shops opening in March 1964.

The start of 1962 saw the Tower Co. make a takeover bid for the Clifton Arms and Pier Hotel Co. Douglas Bickerstaffe appears to have been involved in this because he owned shares in the Clifton Hotel Co. and was a director. However, the other shareholders rejected the Tower bid, which was an all-share bid with no cash (eleven Tower shares for ten Clifton shares). They said they did not see that the Tower was likely to pay a higher dividend than the Clifton, and if they were going to sell, they would prefer to wait for an all cash offer (given that the Tower was listed on the Manchester stock exchange, the last is perhaps a weak argument because it would have been easy to sell the shares). The Clifton Hotel occupied a prominent sea front site opposite the North Pier, but it is not contiguous with the Palace/County Hotel site, even though not far from it. It is not obvious why the Tower would have wanted to buy it, other than to humour Douglas Bickerstaffe. The building is still there but is now an IBIS Styles hotel.

Barry Band says that the Tower Co. also disposed of its three cinemas along the coast from Blackpool at this time.[25] The cinemas, at Lytham, Fleetwood and St Anne's, had never been major generators of profit, but represented John Bickerstaffe's only venture outside the Blackpool heartland, and even then they were also on the Fylde coast.

1962 turned out not to be such a good year for the company – the chairman reported that while conference business had held up, summer visitors were down. For the car dealership he reported a trend towards buying smaller cars, leading to smaller profit margins. He said that the Tower buildings had started a programme of renovation and improvement, which they hoped to complete by 1964.

1963 was better in terms of holiday visitors, but the group result was hit by the reduction in investment income. As the development of the Palace/County Hotel site was proceeding, the group was selling off its financial investments to fund the work. This had two consequences: there was much less interest earned, and gains and losses were recorded on investments.[26] The chairman's report comments that there was a loss of £30,975 on government securities, which had been bought a long time ago (the cynical would say he was pointing out he was not responsible). The sale of trade investments yielded a surplus of £17,535 (these were bought in the late 1950s, so he had been involved). He reported that the company was continuing its programme of improvement and modernisation at the Tower, and the Palace development was coming along with seven out of nine shops pre-let.

For the 1964 season, Dr Badman told shareholders that it had been a good year and the board was able to increase the dividend, even if the late season had been spoiled by the cancellation of three big political conferences as a result of the government's decision to call an election. He reported continuing expenditure on refurbishment of the buildings and expansion of the Winter Gardens site to include a new car showroom. He thanked Douglas Bickerstaffe, who retired from the board that year, for his service, as also J. H. Clegg who had been with the company fifty-one years, eventually as company secretary and then as a director.

The following year saw profits improved by revenue from the Palace/County Hotel development, but it also saw a downturn in the entertainment business, and the dividend was reduced. Dr Badman blamed a government-inspired credit squeeze, but he also noted that the railways had brought one third fewer visitors than the previous year. Part of this was as a result of people travelling by car and coach, and he exhorted Blackpool Council to build more parking facilities. The company had spent a lot of time and money in 1965 fighting a council development proposal for the centre of Blackpool which involved, in Dr Badman's view, the provision of more retail space than was necessary. Long gone were the times when the directors of the Tower Co. also had a significant role in the council's deliberations.

1966 was even worse, with the dividend again reduced. The only good news for the shareholders was that the council had approved a proposal by the company for redeveloping its properties along Central Beach. However, a bombshell was awaiting the shareholders: at the end of the 1967 season, (for which the profits were even lower than in 1966) EMI made a public takeover bid for the Blackpool Tower Co. The *Financial Times* (26 October 1967) reported that the offer valued the Tower Co. shares at 61s (£3.05) representing a premium of about 20 per cent against the market price ahead of the bid. The Tower Co. board recommended that shareholders should accept the offer. The newspaper report commented that it thought that board members controlled about 20 per cent of the shares directly, and could influence probably 60 per cent held by residents in Blackpool and more widely in Lancashire.

People looking at EMI in the twenty-first century think of it as a long-established record company, but in the 1960s and 1970s it was at its peak as a conglomerate. Certainly it was a worldwide recording business featuring among others the Beatles, but the group had extensive electronics and television interests, and in the 1960s a desire to build up a wider entertainment arm, which it did, acquiring ABC Cinemas (then one of the two largest UK chains alongside Odeon) and Thames Television (London weekday franchise producing shows such as The Sweeney and owning Teddington studios). It over-extended itself in the 1980s with the world's first brain scanner, got into difficulties and was taken over by Thorn, which subsequently dismantled the group, selling off many of the constituent businesses, before itself being wiped out by competition from the Far East.

Bernard Delfont

The key mover in the takeover of the Tower Copany was Bernard Delfont. Barry Band devotes a whole chapter to Delfont in his book on the Blackpool Opera House (*The Man Who Would Be King*).[27] Having played Blackpool as a dancer just before the Second World War, Delfont then moved into talent agency and production management. According to Band he put a number of touring shows into Blackpool at both the Opera House and the Grand Theatre during the war and continued to do so thereafter. However, although he was producing in other resorts, it was not until 1957 that he was able to get a Blackpool theatre for a full season, when he took the North Pier. After that the number of productions expanded, including the last two summer seasons at the Palace.

Michael Grade (Lord Grade, Delfont's nephew) said[28] 'There was no question but that summer entertainment was the cornerstone of his business, and he did it very well. He had a good sense of what the public would pay to see, and was good at persuading the artistes to provide it. Blackpool was a major piece of his empire. There was a huge profit to be made in sixteen–eighteen week seasons at theatres like the Opera House. It was a very lucrative business and the shows were truly spectacular. Bernard Delfont was very fond of Blackpool and very instrumental in the Tower Company's acquisition by EMI'

Band says that there was a story circulating in Blackpool in the early part of 1967 that Delfont was going to bid for the Tower Co., but nothing emerged until Delfont fronted the EMI bid in October, having just become a main board director of EMI. The *Financial Times* ran the story on 26 October under the headline 'Mr Delfont brings EMI and Blackpool Tower together'. It confirmed the story that he had made an approach earlier in the year, saying he had withdrawn because the price asked was too high. It quoted him as saying that they did not think they would need to spend money developing the buildings, but EMI had the resources if they were required. He added that the show production experience of the Grade Organisation would benefit the Tower Co., and he had every confidence that the resort of Blackpool would continue to expand.

The *Financial Times* article noted that the only other obvious rivals in the purchase would have been Forte's and Associated Television (ATV), and they had both declared that they were not interested – not too surprising given that Delfont was also a director of Forte's and ATV was run by his brother.

The sale of the Tower Co. to EMI was the end of the company as John Bickerstaffe had created it. Of course the Tower is still there, now owned by Blackpool Council and still operating, but in between 1967 and its acquisition by the council it has been part of a changing set of assets owned by companies whose interests were primarily elsewhere, and whose operating strategy has not been focussed on Blackpool exclusively. For the purposes of this book, in some ways this is the end of the core narrative. The Tower Co. was no longer an independent listed company with a life of its own, but an offshoot of larger empires, and would actually disappear as a legal entity in 1994. We will continue to review its progress, but John Bickerstaffe's company had in effect disappeared.

II

THE DELFONT YEARS

This last phase of the Blackpool Tower Company's life is characterised by moving from a significant local company with local shareholders and board, to being a subsidiary of large companies, with outside management and subject to the vicissitudes of the life of the larger company. The key person in this was Bernard Delfont, although in its last decade the business was also owned by the private investor Trevor Hemmings before being bought by Blackpool Council.

Bernard Delfont was a colourful risk-taker and opportunist who figured large in the British show business and legitimate theatre scene from the 1940s to the 1980s, picking up a knighthood and a peerage on the way. He was the middle brother in a successful show business family. Born Boris Winogradsky in the Ukraine in 1909, he and his elder brother Lewis were brought to England as small children (on arrival his parents changed his name to Barnet). They lived in an immigrant Jewish community in the East End of London[1].

Barnet left school aged twelve and started earning money by winning (and then selling) prizes in competitions for dancing the Charleston, then all the rage. His elder brother, Lew, changed his surname to Grade and became a professional dancer. Barnet soon followed him, doing a speciality double act as Grade and Sutton.[2] This was not too successful and their agent advised them to get a more snappy name for their act, so they became the Delfont Boys.

The two subsequently split up when Sutton married a dancer and decided they were better off not splitting the fees with

Barnet. Delfont retained the name (although sometimes still calling himself Grade in his private life), and spent some time in the 1930s looking for work in theatres and night clubs all over northern Europe. In Brussels he met a Eurasian girl dancer called Toko, and they teamed up as a new double act (Toko's English mum came too). It was as Delfont and Toko that he appeared in Blackpool at the Palace in 1937 and 1938.

Lew Grade, who appears to have been more successful as a dancer than Delfont, had by this time abandoned the stage to set up a talent agency. Delfont decided in 1939, aged thirty, that his body was no longer up to the twice-nightly exotic dance routine and decided to follow his elder brother into management. He was given space in his brother's firm (Collins & Grade), but within months they parted, not on the friendliest of terms, because Delfont wanted to run his own business.

Delfont was not that keen on the agency business; he wanted to be a producer and theatre manager, but being a talent agent was the easiest route into management in the theatre because all that was needed was a telephone, a contacts book and an extensive knowledge of show business. By discovering a new talent and signing them up, the agent's fortune would grow with theirs. The agent could also leverage engagements for lesser acts on the back of the main attraction. The 'star' would also give the agent leverage to win theatre leases and production deals. Delfont in fact was lucky in that he found a pianist, Charlie Kunz, who did a variety act and whose career took off in Delfont's hands.

Delfont quickly decided to hire someone to run his talent agency, so that he could get on with production. He hired young Billy Marsh, who would turn out to be one of the most successful agents in the business in Britain, and whose clients would later include Norman Wisdom, Morecambe and Wise and Cliff Richard. Billy Marsh and Keith Devon ran Delfont's agency and made it a dominant force in variety.

Of course the war intervened very early in the evolution of Delfont's management career. He had a stroke of fortune that while he and his two brothers were called up to do military service, he was then rejected as being a foreigner. Leslie Grade, the youngest of the three by a margin, had been born in England, and was sent to the RAF. Lew Grade had been naturalised, and was also taken, even if he was ultimately invalided out of the army.

Delfont, however, had not bothered to apply for naturalisation. As he explains in his book, it cost money, which for him was always in short supply, and he had been able to travel around Europe in the 1930s without difficulty using his stateless person papers. The recruiters said he could not go into the forces.

He was therefore free to continue his theatrical career, and because of the war, there were cheap deals to be had both for renting theatres and acquiring scenery and costumes at knock-down prices. The established promoters were chary of the war time conditions, and some had moved to places like Blackpool. By the end of 1939 Delfont had put together a variety show that did a provincial tour, and by 1942 he had productions in West End theatres and shows touring the provinces.

After the war, Lew Grade wound up his Collins and Grade agency and joined up with the youngest brother, Leslie Grade, to form Lew & Leslie Grade Ltd. Leslie Grade preferred to leave the limelight to his two deal-maker brothers, and concentrated on the agency business. Lew Grade saw the potential of the new independent television service and set up a consortium to bid for the franchises that were being offered. In 1955 he left Lew & Leslie Grade Ltd to be head of Associated Television (ATV) which was to be his powerhouse for the rest of his career.

1955 sticks in Michael Grade's memory as being a year when the Royal Variety Performance was at the Blackpool Opera House. He recalls: 'I went to the Royal Variety performance in Blackpool in 1955 when I was a kid. I remember going in to see the rehearsals, but what fascinated me was the information that the theatre had had to build a loo just behind the royal box, for the use of the queen. What interested me most was to know whether it had been used.'

Delfont meanwhile ploughed his own furrow, doing many theatrical productions, both straight plays and variety and sea side summer season shows. He also got control of some London theatres, eventually including the Prince of Wales Theatre which was to be his base for many years. At the time the Stoll Theatres and Moss Empires touring circuits were still going strong, and he regularly sent touring shows round.

He discovered that Moss Empires might be willing to sell the lease of the Hippodrome Theatre, on the edge of Leicester Square and Charing Cross Road, and had the idea of turning it into a variety theatre where people could also have dinner. However, aside from mounting an extravagant show, he needed money to convert the interior of the theatre so that there was a dance floor and flat surfaces for the dining tables.

By chance he mentioned this to an old acquaintance, one Charles Forte whom he had got to know when they were both starting out, because out-of-work actors used to meet in cafés, including Forte's first milk bar, which opened in 1935 (the Strand Milk Bar, in Regent Street). Like Delfont, Forte had moved on a long way and was now able to offer him all the money he needed. Forte would provide the catering, Delfont the shows: the Talk of the Town opened in 1958. It became a money-spinner for Delfont, and a flagship for his variety productions, and he remained a key partner for Forte in the latter's ambitions to expand into entertainment. When Forte took his company public, Delfont was named a main board director. He was subsequently instrumental in Forte buying each of Blackpool's three piers, starting with the North Pier.

Leslie Grade had also been expanding, acquiring other talent agencies, as well as Shipman and King, a thirty-odd cinema circuit in the South East corner of England. Eventually he approached

Delfont about buying Delfont's agency, still run by Billy Marsh and Keith Devon. Delfont finally agreed, but in exchange for a shareholding in what was now called the Grade Organisation. Delfont continued to run his productions from the Prince of Wales, but his agency moved to Regent House, at the top of Regent Street, with Leslie's other agencies.

This was to change dramatically in 1966 when Leslie had a stroke. Delfont says in his autobiography that his younger brother had been frail ever since he returned from war service. It seemed clear that after the stroke he would never return to manage the Grade Organisation, and so Delfont took a more prominent role in the management. He also moved into the company Leslie's son Michael, then aged twenty-four.

At the same time, EMI was talking to the brothers about making a bid for the Grade Organisation. As mentioned earlier, the EMI of 1966 was a much bigger and more complex company than the EMI of 2016, which is more or less a recording company only. In those days records were of course important to the company, but it was also extensively involved in electronics (defence electronics, television studios, computers and latterly medical electronics) as well as some manufacturing of white goods.

It was more fashionable then than now to be a 'conglomerate' with a range of often unrelated businesses under the same umbrella – General Electric and United Technologies in the US are the two most prominent companies that have been able to survive and thrive with such a business model. At the time the company was doing well and had money to invest by diversifying in the entertainment industry from which it hoped to gain synergies.[3]

This was a big decision for Delfont. On the one hand, in light of Leslie's stroke, a sale might be a good thing, but on the other, EMI did not just want the company, they wanted Delfont to head their new leisure division. He was going to have to cease being an independent producer and become a corporate executive.

He asked an outrageous price for the shares in the Grade Organisation, and EMI just wrote him a cheque. He says in his autobiography:

> I would enjoy unrivalled opportunities to build up the leisure division into a major company in its own right. There was no shortage of investment money and I would have virtually a free hand on how to spend it. It was an offer I could not resist.[4]

He goes on: 'I started off at EMI in pursuit of a love affair. I had always had a soft spot for Blackpool'. He says that at its worst it was seedy and decrepit – cheap charter flights to the European sunspots had hit hard and many once-prosperous coastal towns looked to be in terminal decline. But Blackpool was an exception, the resort was held in enormous affection by millions of holidaymakers. He notes that after negotiating the purchase of the North Pier for Charles Forte's company, he had invested Forte's money in the property and transformed it with the addition of more facilities and then staged top variety shows and the business had thrived.

Delfont adds: 'The prospect that caused me greatest excitement was the Blackpool Tower Co. One only had to glance at their property portfolio to realise that their shares were much undervalued' (p176). In the event Delfont approached Dr Badman, observing in his autobiography that Badman was an anaesthetist and Delfont felt 'his commitment to his part time job was less than whole-hearted'. Delfont did not feel they could meet too publicly because that would cause speculation, so the deal was done over four meetings in the buffet at Crewe railway station.

Delfont says they agreed a price of £4,600,000, adding 'both of us were empowered to shake on the deal there and then'. That has to be an over-simplification in that while Delfont may have had the authority from the EMI board, the Tower Co. was a listed company with no dominant shareholder, so the chairman could not close a deal definitively, the shareholders had to agree to sell their shares. No doubt he had the board's authority to negotiate, and they backed the price he had agreed, but they still needed shareholders to vote. As mentioned in the previous chapter, the *Financial Times* (26 October 1967) said the board spoke for 20 per cent of the votes and was thought to be able to influence another 60 per cent held by residents of Blackpool and Lancashire more generally.

Michael Grade says: 'Blackpool was thriving right through the 1960s and 1970s. It did not start to decline until the very end of the 1970s. Weekly variety had started to decline long before, but the long seasons at Blackpool did not decline till much later.

An EMI Subsidiary

The general rule when a larger company takes over a smaller one is that the key personnel of the acquisition are changed, and management is sent in from the new parent. However, in the case of the Blackpool Tower Co., both Ted Badman, the chairman, and Donald Gledhill, the general manager retained their jobs and their seats on the board. It was quite in Delfont's style to keep Gledhill in place to do the day to day running, just as Delfont worked with people like Billy Marsh and Richard Mills running parts of the Grade Organisation. Possibly Badman was kept in place as a nod to the Blackpool business community, or he had negotiated that as part of the sale to EMI.

However, Bernard Delfont and John Read (the chief executive of EMI at the time) also went on the board and the non-executive directors left the company. Subsequently Delfont appointed Dickie Hurran to the Tower Co. board. Hurran was a show director who had overseen many of Delfont's variety shows for years, and according to Delfont's biography, was put in to keep an eye on the circus. Leslie Grade was also briefly put on the Tower board, but stepped down in 1970.

One of the unintended consequences of the EMI takeover was that the Tower Company's financial year-end was moved from 31 October to 30 June. The auditors were also changed, and while Thomas Smethurst was long dead, his successors, now operating as part of Whinney Murray, had continued to audit the company. 1967 was to be the last year of the association, which dated back to 1891. Cooper Brothers (now part of PricewaterhouseCoopers) were the auditors for EMI and were immediately given the Tower audit, as is still common practice. Just as investors prefer 'consolidated' financial statements so you can see the whole group, there is a fear that if you have different auditors for different parts of the group, something may drop through a crack.[6]

The change in accounting date was clearly ridiculous for a company whose activities mostly took place between April and October, but was unavoidable because of the accounting rules. When one company controls another, aside from the individual company annual financial statements, the parent has to produce the set of consolidated financial statements. These statements, group accounts, aggregate the financial data of all the companies controlled by the parent. The accounting requirements at the time said that as far as possible, all the subsidiaries should have the same year-end, so that the consolidated statements related to the same period for each company. The only thing EMI could have done was to change the group year-end, which it was unlikely to do for a minor sub-group.

The Grade Organisation had the same problem – in the acquisition by EMI, Delfont's summer show producing activity had been rolled in to the deal, and the producing companies were busy writing 30 June financial statements for activities which ran principally from June to September, and whose outcome was unknown until October.

From a research perspective, the change of year-end also makes it very difficult to analyse the Tower Company's accounts. In 1968 they switched to the 30 June year-end, reporting figures for eight months only in the 1968 statements.[7] It is therefore not possible to compare the subsequent performance of the company with the pre-EMI performance. The other issue is that once the Tower Co. was part of a bigger group, some of its transactions would no longer be at arms' length.

In particular, in the EMI years, the Grade Organisation became the biggest producer of shows at Tower Co. venues. There is no reason to suppose that the contractual terms were any different than they would have been to independent producers, but once one subsidiary contracts with another, the exact split of profits becomes of only theoretical interest, since it all remains within the same group. There are also casual cross-subsidies where, for example, EMI might get free publicity when the Tower Co. was advertising shows, or the Tower Co. received the benefit of show business expertise without paying for it.

What is clear is that once EMI had the Tower Co., Delfont produced or was involved in most of the large shows in Blackpool. A 1969 advertisement, reproduced on the dust cover of Delfont's autobiography, credits him with shows that summer at not only the Opera House, Grand Theatre, Winter Gardens Pavilion and Tower Circus, but also at the North Pier, the Central Pier and the ABC cinema (which at the time included a stage and the equipment necessary to mount live shows as well as films).

The presence of the ABC is as a result of Delfont's continued activity in investing EMI's money. In 1968, Delfont bid to acquire the Associated British Picture Corporation (ABPC). This company was the second largest British film producer after Rank, and also owned the 350 ABC cinemas, Elstree Film Studios, and a half interest in Thames Television, which then had the London weekday franchise and is remembered for programmes like 'The Sweeney'. EMI eventually succeeded in its bid, and ABPC became the EMI Film and Theatre Corporation, Bernard Delfont became its chairman and chief executive.

Government competition authorities were not keen on this, and the newspapers pointed out that EMI controlled the largest talent agencies, big show producers running most of the large summer variety shows, West End theatres, film production, a large cinema chain and a television company, and suggesting that they would have a stranglehold on the creative industry. The hysteria got even louder when people recognised the family connection to Delfont's brother Lew, who controlled more West End theatres and another large television company.

It probably makes entertaining newspaper copy, but suggesting that two public companies might somehow combine informally to control an industry is a bit far-fetched, especially when the two brothers did not get on especially well and did not socialise with each other. It also overstates the extent to which the EMI companies dominated the market. However, the government intervened and EMI was obliged to hive off the talent agencies which reverted to being a private group.

They kept the Grade Organisation as such, which moved into Delfont's old offices in the Prince of Wales Theatre, with Richard Mills in charge, while Delfont himself moved to ABPC's office in Golden Square (just to the East of Regent Street). Richard Mills had been Delfont's head of production for some time and continued to oversee variety and pantomime production as well as West End shows and theatres.

Grand Theatre

As discussed earlier, this was a period when theatre was in decline. Where the Tower Co. had been able to keep some of its facilities open all year round with both live shows and films in the late 1940s and early 1950s, increasingly there was not a large enough audience in the winter to justify this. Similarly when the big shows were at their peak, the cast might have done twice nightly Monday to Saturday, and with two matinees as well; the matinees fell away, and then on some nights there was only one performance.

In the early 1970s it became clear that the Grand Theatre was having difficulty remaining profitable. It seats about 1,100 people, which makes it unsuitable for a big variety show, where a producer would want as near 2,000 seats as possible. Consequently it was more often used for plays, but provincial theatre and the touring circuits had virtually disappeared after the advent of television, and there was neither an audience for this kind of entertainment nor a wide choice of product.

At the same time, Blackpool Council was thinking about redeveloping the area around the Grand. This idea had been around since the 1960s, at the time when Douglas Bickerstaffe and Ted Badman had knocked down the Palace and built a department store. It had been temporarily shelved, but it came back again, and the Tower Co. was giving serious thought to demolishing the Grand Theatre as well and developing more retail space as part of the town centre redevelopment plan.

Barry Band reports that as early as 1971 a member of the Victorian Society had suggested listing the building after seeing its interior. Some Blackpool residents concerned about its future had it listed in 1972. It became a protected building and when the Tower Co. later suggested development, residents were able to mobilise opposition to the proposal and demand a public hearing.

The Tower Co. then came up with the idea of turning it into a bingo hall. The Friends of the Grand, formed to protect the theatre, mobilised again and came up with a plan for leasing the theatre for £10,000 a year, and eventually the theatre was sold to The Grand Theatre Trust in 1980. Although the theatre was preserved, for the Tower Co. it was not its most glorious moment, and represented the second significant disposal from the imposing set of entertainment establishments that John Bickerstaffe had built up.

Problems at EMI

Delfont's attention, to judge from his autobiography, seems to have been largely focused on making films after EMI acquired ABPC, with Donald Gledhill running the Tower Co. and Richard Mills the Grade Organisation. However, Delfont's attention came back to his theatrical interests at the end of the 1970s. He had built up EMI Film & Theatre Corporation to be a significant contributor to group profit, but the conglomerate was holed below the waterline by a brain scanner.

Innovation in electronics had been a big part of the company's past – for example the 405 line television broadcast system used by the UK until the arrival of colour television in the 1960s had been invented by EMI. The company got involved in medical electronics and invented the world's first brain scanner. This was a big money-spinner in the first instance, but as Delfont tells it, they were approached by an American company who asked for a licence to develop the scanner. EMI refused, so the company developed its own scanner and eventually the previously lucrative US markets closed to EMI, preferring an American supplier.[8]

The medical electronics division had scaled up production rapidly, and now was deflated quickly, leaving the EMI group with massive debts and in need of a white knight. Thorn's 1979 takeover bid succeeded and although their declared intention was to expand the company, in 1980 they started to sell off bits of EMI. Delfont succeeded in selling the Tower Co. and the Grade Organisation to Charles Forte's company, now called Trusthouse Forte (THF). The package included a number of non-related assets such as a marina at Chichester, a sports division and ballrooms. The *Financial Times* reported that a group of Blackpool businessmen asked for the deal to be referred to the Monopolies Commission, as they were miffed that a bid they had mounted for the Tower Co. was rejected by EMI.

Delfont (who was knighted in 1974 and made a life peer by Harold Wilson in his resignation honours in 1976) says in his autobiography (p209) that 'leisure was not a core activity' for Thorn and Delfont felt that they should not let that side of the business prevent them from expanding the electronics and records side. He sold the hotels division for Thorn but the chairman of Thorn then called him when on holiday to point out that Delfont was approaching his seventieth birthday, and would have to step down from the board under Thorn's rules. Delfont was not very pleased about something that had never been mentioned in any previous discussions, and went to talk to Charles Forte.

As he says, they had worked together for more than twenty years in the Talk of the Town venture. Delfont had subsequently bought Blackpool properties for Forte's leisure division and now proposed that the Tower Co., all Delfont's old production and West Efnd theatre activities and various sports ventures be sold to THF for £14 million. Forte agreed on condition that the properties were merged into THF's leisure division with Delfont as chairman and chief executive of that division.

Delfont seemed set to carry on with his theatrical career, but his time at THF was to be limited. In 1982 he was taken on one side by one of Forte's senior aides and was told that Charles Forte was to step down as chief executive and pass the management of the group to his son Rocco Forte. Rocco had concentrated throughout his career on the hotel side, and was not interested in developing the leisure division. Delfont reports (p211) that he subsequently had a conversation with Charles Forte who said that if Delfont was against selling the leisure division, that view would be respected. Delfont however decided that it would be better to go, and set about trying to raise money to buy THF Leisure himself.

This he succeeded in doing, creating First Leisure and agreeing to buy THF Leisure for £43.5 million. The *Financial Times* of 11 December 1982 quoted Donald Durban, a director of THF, as saying: 'We think we are quite good at hotels and catering and should concentrate on doing the things we are best at. The leisure division is a very good one. We are happy to sell it to Lord Delfont, who has been on our board for twenty years, but if anything went wrong with the deal we should also be happy to keep it.'

The article notes that the division made profits of £8.9 million the previous year, but that this included profits on property disposals, and the underlying profit was thought to be £4 million a year. The Lex column on the same day suggested that the price was a very respectable exit for THF, representing about 15 times historic earnings. It adds: 'Dolphinaria and amusement parks have never looked quite comfortable sandwiched between THF's far larger catering and hotel interests so the proposed sale ... makes eminent strategic sense.'

First Leisure's main backer was London Merchant Securities, a property group, but other backers included Refuge Assurance, Norwich Union, Eagle Star and Royal Insurance. The portfolio First Leisure acquired included the Tower Co. and the Grade Organisation and other assets Delfont had taken in from EMI, but also THF's other leisure assets, including the three Blackpool piers, a dolphinarium, Summerland (an entertainment centre in the Isle of Man), a holiday village in St Ives, a caravan park and various assets such as discos, squash clubs and bowling clubs. The Lex column described the assets as 'a real ragbag' but said they were more appropriate to the kind of 'entrepreneurial management which Lord Delfont will doubtless bring to bear.'

The *Financial Times* also ran a background piece on the same day which commented: 'Many of the assets Delfont is likely to acquire ... have been part of his empire for some years. The only changes have been the corporate banner on the door.' The article adds that 'under both EMI and THF his office and administration have been kept at arms' length from the parental base and thus easily mobile.'

In March 1984 Delfont took First Leisure public, with an offering of £10 million of shares. The *Financial Times* reported that the offer was oversubscribed more than thirty times, with applications for £350 million of shares. The newspaper quoted Delfont as saying that the British seaside was far from dead, in spite of the popularity of overseas holidays. He added that the development of motorways was making it more accessible to day-trippers. Profits from the piers increased every year, he said.

Barry Band[9] reports that First Leisure held its annual shareholders' meeting in Blackpool in 1984, and quotes Delfont as saying 'Some of the directors have not been to Blackpool before, and I want them to share the enthusiasm I have for what is the premier resort in the country.' The company also set out on a programme of refurbishment, starting with the Tower buildings and the South and Central piers, and then moving on to the Winter Gardens and the North Pier. Band says that the Opera House was refurbished in 1987 as part of a £4 million redevelopment of the Winter Gardens site, but is critical of what he saw as the limited extent of this. Delfont stood down as executive chairman of First Leisure in 1988 but remained president of the company.

1994 marked the centenary of the opening of the Tower[10], and the occasion was used as a marketing platform. However, the year also included in July the death of Bernard Delfont, aged 84, of a heart attack. Band (p68) comments that from 1994 the rumours were rife about the future attitude of First Leisure to the resort: 'Would the new management have Bernie's love of Blackpool?'

In fact Michael Grade was appointed non-executive chairman of First Leisure at the beginning of 1995, and then in 1997 stepped down from running Channel Four and took over the running of First Leisure full time. Band says: 'He was not as stage struck as his Uncle Bernie and eventually decided that the company's future was in building up its empire of health and fitness centres.' (p69). The *Financial Times* commented in 1997 that in the previous year growth in the nightclubs, health and fitness businesses had been offset by falling profits from bingo and theatres. It notes profits were £43.7 million on a turnover of £183 million, but adds: 'City analysts were disappointed and dubbed the company "Old Leisure", something that Mr Grade, with his instinct for popular taste, should be able to do something about.'

Michael Grade commented for this book: '[First Leisure] needed massive capital expenditure and profits were declining every year. We were a diverse entertainment conglomerate but in all the areas I could not see any future. I could see changes coming which would damage the business. We made money from premises with late night licenses, but licensing was about to be opened up. Smoking bans were on the way. It was time to get money back for the investors.'

The Times reported in September 1998 that First Leisure had sold 'the bulk of its resorts division' for £74 million to Leisure Parcs Ltd, a company in which the family interests of Trevor Hemmings had a controlling stake. The newspaper adds that the deal included the Blackpool Tower, but not the caravan park in Wales, considered to be the division's most profitable business.

The *Daily Express* reported: 'Trevor Hemmings, the multimillionaire who built the Pontin's holiday group, yesterday fulfilled a childhood dream with the acquisition of Blackpool Tower.' It adds: 'Hemmings is reported to have promised on family holidays that he would one day be rich enough to buy the resort he loved.' The deal included the Winter Gardens and the piers as well as piers in Llandudno and Southsea. Band notes (p69) that after thirty years under the control of London-based companies, the business was back under North-West ownership.

Michael Grade said: 'I went to see Trevor Hemmings. We sat in his kitchen and had a cup of tea, and I sold all the Blackpool business to him. I think his strategy was that he could see gambling coming to Blackpool – it could become the Atlantic City of the north.'

Although the purchase by Leisure Parcs Ltd marked a return to its roots for the Tower Co., and release from being a small part of a much larger and diverse empire, the demand for theatres and show productions in Blackpool was continuing to decline. Barry Band[11] reports that the 1999 summer season show at the Opera House was a flop and an eight week run of Tim Rice and Andrew Lloyd Webber's *Jesus Christ Superstar* in the Christmas season was 'too ambitious'.

The following seasons were more successful but the general manager, Michael Williams, interviewed by Barry Band in 2005, said that competition for acts and shows had become more difficult because of the arrival of American entertainment companies, the promotion of theatres by municipalities and the expansion of city Arena venues. Mr Williams said that summer season shows were no longer an option, and the Opera House would switch to one night touring shows.

In 2009 Leisure Parcs announced that the Winter Gardens complex was losing money and needed massive investment if it was to survive. In fact in the same year the Opera House once again hosted the Royal Variety performance, but that was in effect running counter to the trend. In 2010 the Tower Co. was sold to the Blackpool Council for £40 million[12] and the council then appointed Merlin Entertainments to run it.

Conclusion

The Delfont years provided Blackpool with many great shows, but from about 1955 resort business generally, and entertainment specifically, was changing radically. People went to the theatre less and eventually practised ballroom dancing hardly at all. Blackpool had to downsize its facilities, which it did, starting with the Palace. But people were also taking their summer holidays in hotter climates, and there was also therefore a much smaller audience, and a pattern of people coming to the resort for short stays, often outside the traditional summer season. Blackpool has been able to survive better than many resorts, given its leading position, but it is very different now from its 1950s heyday.

The Blackpool Tower Co. as such survived for more than 100 years (although no-one celebrated its centenary in 1991, even if the laying of the foundation stone was commemorated that year). There is no doubt that it owed its existence to John Bickerstaffe, without whom the project would likely have sunk like so many of William Darker Pitt's seaside money-making schemes. By chance Bickerstaffe had the conviction that it would succeed and also had the connections and resources to build the Tower, even if it was 'a close run thing'.

Thereafter he had a clear policy to ensure that it was always top quality, and the ambition to expand, taking in the bankrupt Alhambra and turning it into the profitable Palace, and then the Grand Theatre, setting up cinemas along the coast, and then finally taking over the Winter Gardens Co. and establishing a commercial cash generator that dominated Blackpool.

When he died in 1930, he left a thriving company which was the premier business in Blackpool. One can see that the management subsequent to him did not succeed in expanding the company. It became a 'cash cow' surviving the depression of the 1930s, doing well in the Second World War but paying massive taxes, and enjoying the post war boom in resort business, until the decline started in the late 1950s.

As often happens when thriving companies start to lose their way, the company was snapped up by a much larger predator in the late 1960s. It continued to put on quality entertainment, but this was a period of change and decline of the traditional offerings, leading eventually to the move from the private sector to the public sector.

NOTES

I

1. E.g Cyril Bainbridge (1986) *Pavilions on the Sea – a history of the seaside pleasure pier,* London, Robert Hale, p19–20.

2. A bathing machine was a small hut on wheels which was pushed down to the water's edge. The bather entered on the landside, changed into swimming gear, and then went down steps into the sea at the opposite end.

3. Bainbridge, op. cit., p212–214.

4. The Entertainments Tax was levied from 1916 to 1960, and was a levy on admissions to all places of entertainment – see Rutterford J. & Walton P 'The War, the Entertainments Tax and the Blackpool Tower Co.' (2014) *Accounting History Review.*

5. John K. Walton (1998) Blackpool Edinburgh University Press/Carnegie Publishing Edinburgh/Lancaster p6 (John Walton – no relation – is a leading social historian with a specialist interest in resorts in general and Blackpool in particular).

6. Victoria and Albert Museum website (http://www.vam.ac.uk/content/articles/v/variety-theatre/) consulted on 28 March 2013.

7. Victoria and Albert Museum as above.

8. Op. cit. p1

9. Op. cit. p2

10. Brian Turner and Steve Palmer (1994) *The Blackpool Story* 3rd edition, Blackpool Corporation, p12.

11. On a personal note, I decided to stay at the North Euston Hotel in Fleetwood during one of my research visits to Blackpool. Ironically, the

visitor to Fleetwood is now invited to take the Blackpool train and get off at Poulton and take a taxi to Fleetwood.

12. Op. cit. p15.

13. Op. cit. p7

14. Op. cit. p26

2

1. Brian Turner and Steve Palmer (1994) *The Blackpool Story* 3rd Edition, Blackpool Corporation, pp24–25.

2. The *Blackpool Gazette* of 15 November 1989 says he was a shareholder in Raikes Hall Gardens, which is probably what was being referred to here.

3. At the time the councillors had the right to appoint several aldermen, people who sat on the council but did not represent a ward and had no popular mandate. Often these were people who had already done good service for the council. Their term of office was normally six years, but, as in Bickerstaffe's case, could be renewed indefinitely.

3

1. FK Pearson (1969) 'The Douglas Head Suspension Bridge' *Journal of the Manx Museum*, Vol VII no 85, pp100–107.

2. The precise relationship between the directors of a company and the chairman varies significantly from one company to another. Legally the company is run by the board of directors, and one of them is appointed chairman. Normally that person should chair meetings but also act as a figurehead. There may be another director who actually runs the day to day operations, but that is not necessarily the case. The Blackpool Tower Co. under John Bickerstaffe was run by a general manager who was not a director. Directors fall into two categories: executive and non-executive. Executive directors work for the company and make day to day decisions about its management. Non-executive directors may represent large shareholdings or be experts or people of influence, who only attend formal meetings.

3. FK Pearson op. cit.

4. The *Blackpool Gazette* commented (19 Dec 1990) that Dr Cocker had put together the properties for a total of £22,800, so the deal represented a

significant profit to him. However the paper took this is part as evidence of the rapid rise in Blackpool property prices as the resort became more popular.

5. Brian Turner and Steve Palmer (1994) *The Blackpool Story* 3rd edition, Corporation of Blackpool, p46.

6. A debenture in this context is a form of mortgage where the money is raised by public subscription rather than from a single lender. If people bought part of the debenture, they would get a guaranteed rate of return (5 per cent in this case) but they would also have the security of being able to take over the company's property if it defaulted on the payments. The investor had a choice between the ordinary share with a forecast return of 8 per cent, but the risk of nothing, and a piece of the debenture at 5 per cent with back-up security.

7. For the investment in assets to cost much more than originally estimated is not exactly a rare phenomenon, but securities regulation has changed a great deal since those days, and a modern prospectus would include supporting reports by experts and penalties for giving misleading information.

8. George Hobbs (2015) *By Whing to Port Soderick – the story of the Manx Marine Drive*, Loaghtan Books, Maughold, Isle of Man.

4

1. Before the UK decimalised in 1971, the pound was divided into 20s, and each shilling into 12d, so there were 240d to the pound. A sum such as 3s and 6d would be written 3/6.

2. He had accepted appointment as mayor of Blackpool for a second year.

3. Since people had only to put up 5 per cent of the price at the beginning, there was the risk that they would not have the means to pay the remaining instalments.

4. The market takes the view that £100 received today, is worth more than £100 received in a year's time. Supposing you can earn interest at 5 per cent per annum, if you have £100 today, it will be worth £105 in a year. Conversely if you are to receive £100 in a year, it is worth only £95 today. This is called the time value of money, and you deduct this (called discounting) to assess competing investments that have different cash flows.

An investment that offers you £100 in a year's time is worth more than a competing investment that offers you £102 in two years' time.

5. It is not clear how and when this came in to being. The minutes of Blackpool Council's Finance Committee for 15 October 1891 show agreement that the Tower Co. should take over responsibility for a £25,000 mortgage given to Blackpool Central Promenade Estates Ltd, and a further £5,000 was paid to the Tower Co. in July 1892. We have not been able to discover any more about Blackpool Central Promenade Estates, but a possible explanation is that the £25,000 mortgage related to Dr Cocker's Aquarium and Beach Hotel, and Bickerstaffe negotiated with the Council to take over the debt instead of paying Dr Cocker in cash.

6. Edgar Jones (1891) *Accountancy and the British Economy 1840–1980, the evolution of Ernst and Whinney Batsford*, London.

5

1. It became part of the EMI Group in 1967, after which separate figures are not available.

2. Brian Hornsey (1994*) Ninety years of cinema in Blackpool*, Fuchsiaprint, p5.

3. Bill Curtis (1988) *Blackpool Tower*, Lavenham, Terence Dalton Ltd, p38.

4. Vanessa Toulmin (2011), *Blackpool Tower*, Blackpool Council.

5. Brian Turner & Steve Palmer (1994), *The Blackpool Story 3rd edition*, Blackpool Council.

6. Turner and Palmer say that promoter William Porter bought the land for £120,000 and then sold it to the Alhambra Co. for £224,000.

7. Given that the company had issued shares for about £35,000 to finance the refurbishment of the Tower buildings three years before, the new financing would return the Company to its approximately 50/50 debt/equity split.

8. Op. cit. p61

9. Op. cit. p44

10. Nowadays a company making such an acquisition would probably have accounted for the acquired company as a subsidiary. Bickerstaffe seems to have preferred not to have any subsidiaries and instead take the assets and liabilities of the acquired company directly into the Tower Co. balance sheet. A side effect of this is that there would have been no independent valuation of

the acquisition and no clue as to whether Bickerstaffe had paid a premium to acquire the theatre.

6

1. The 1907 Companies Act required companies to file annual financial statements at Companies House, and from 1909 these are still available to be consulted in the Blackpool Tower Co. file. Very much shorter than today's financial statements – there were no notes to the accounts in 1909 – these tended to be a single large sheet of paper pasted in to the annual return.

2. The company could not vary the interest paid on its debentures and other borrowing, but it could in those days choose how much depreciation it charged, or what deductions were made for 'reserves', so this figure is a better index of relative performance than net earnings after depreciation, tax and interest.

3. Janette Rutterford and Peter Walton 'The War, Taxation and the Blackpool Tower Co.', *Accounting History Review*, 2014.

4. Rutterford and Walton op. cit.

5. This is a little bit of a simplification, and anyone wanting to delve into it is recommended to try Rutterford and Walton.

6. The link between reported profit and dividend disappeared some decades ago. Shareholders look typically for a continuing or enhanced level of dividend, without regard to the reported profit.

7. This is a subtle manoeuvre to lock the reserves in to the company's capital structure. By issuing shares free of charge, the shareholders felt they were getting something worthwhile and they could always sell some shares if they needed cash, but the reserves, which had started out as part of the operating profit, were now part of the permanent capital and could not be paid out subsequently in dividend.

7

1. Barry Band (2012) *The Main Stage*, published by Mr Band, in Blackpool, is a history of the development of the Winter Gardens. Mr Band says (p1) that 'Business leaders and developers all over Britain had been influenced by the visual attraction and the success of London's Crystal Palace. Glass-covered

"winter gardens" and shopping arcades were opening in cities and large towns.""

2. Brian Turner and Steve Palmer (1994) *The Blackpool Story* 3rd edition Blackpool Corporation, pp29–30.

3. Turner and Palmer op. cit. p38.

4. Vanessa Toulmin (2011) *The Blackpool Tower*, Boco Publishing, p71.

5. Barry Band (2012) reports (p14) that Mrs Huddlestone was born Frieda Rocca Kaczka 'a member of a family of theatrical entrepreneurs' that John Huddlestone had met in Nice. Mr Band notes that, to the astonishment of many, Mr Huddlestone, then aged forty-seven, married his wife in 1908, when he had already spent twenty-five years in the service of the Winter Gardens Co. He says 'Mrs Frieda Huddlestone quickly became a popular figure in Blackpool social circles.'

6. Barry Band (2012) says that Frederick Badman was a Birmingham man who had bought shares in the Winter Gardens Co. and in the difficult time for the company in the 1890s was a frequent complainant about the company's performance. He was appointed a director in 1895. His family were to continue to play a significant role in Blackpool affairs, including his grandson being made chairman of the Tower Co. in 1961.

7. Sue Arthur (2012) *Popular Entertainment in 1930s Blackpool*, Doctoral thesis, Leeds Metropolitan University.

8. The Tower had an enquiries telephone number: Blackpool 1.

9. Bernard Crabtree (2002) *That was showbiz* published by Barry Band (Publishing), Blackpool.

8

1. John Walton (1998) *Blackpool*, Edinburgh University Press/Carnegie Publishing, Lancaster, pp80–86.

2. Sue Arthur (2013) *Popular Entertainment in 1930s Blackpool*, Doctoral Thesis, Leeds Metropolitan University.

3. James Foreman Peck (1995) *A History of the World Economy* 2nd edition, Harvester Wheatsheaf, Hemel Hempstead, p233.

4. Brian Turner and Steve Palmer (1994) *The Blackpool Story* 3rd Edition Blackpool Corporation, p117.

5. Barry Band (2005) *The Main Stage* Barry Band, Blackpool.

6. Op. cit.

7. Barry Band (2012) *Blackpool's Palace Theatre*, Band, Blackpool, p12.

9

1. Brian Turner and Steve Palmer (1994) *The Blackpool Story 3rd Edition* Blackpool Corporation, p124.

2. J.R. Hicks, U.K. Hicks & L. Rostas (1941) *The Taxation of War Wealth*, Oxford, Clarendon Press, pp93–103.

3. Martin Daunton (2002) *Just taxes: the politics of taxation in Britain 1914–1979*, Cambridge, pp176–214.

4. John Walton (1998) *Blackpool*, Carnegie/Edinburgh University Press p135

5. Barry Band (2005) *The Main Stage*, Blackpool, pp27–31.

10

1. John Walton (1998) *Blackpool*, University of Edinburgh Press/Carnegie , p141.

2. Barry Band 2012 *Blackpool's Palace Theatre*. p17.

3. Martin Daunton (2002) *Just taxes: the politics of taxation in Britain 1914–1979*, Cambridge.

4. Bill Curtis (1988) *Blackpool Tower*, Terence Dalton, Lavenham, p66.

5. Walton, ibid, p139.

6. Brian Turner and Steve Palmer (1994) *The Blackpool Story 3rd Edition*, Blackpool Corporation, p133/134.

7. Barry Band 2012 *Blackpool's Palace Theatre*, p17.

8. Curtis, ibid, p67.

9. One of the more prominent involved Robert Maxwell. He had a publishing company that was sold to an American investor. Prior to the sale a lot of books had been sold to another Maxwell Co., thus boosting profits in the publisher. The sales stopped when the publisher was sold. The investor subsequently sued, having been unaware of the link.

10. Curtis, ibid, p113.

11. Curtis, ibid, p114.

12. Band (2012), p17/18.

13. Bernard Crabtree (2002) *That was showbiz* Barry Band (Publishing) Blackpool, p29.

14. Curtis ibid, p101.

15. Vanessa Toulmin (2011) *Blackpool Tower*, Blackpool Council, p88.

16. Turner & Palmer ibid, p134.

17. Crabtree (2002), p20.

18. The *Gazette*, announcing the development in March 1961, said that Lewis's was started by one David Lewis in 1856 with a small shop in Liverpool. A store was opened in Manchester in 1880 and another in Birmingham in 1885. After David Lewis's death, further stores followed in Glasgow, Leeds, Hanley, Leicester and Bristol, and the company eventually acquired Selfridge's in Oxford Street, London.

19. Barry Band (2012), *Blackpool's Palace Theatre*, p1.

20. Barry Band (2005) *The Main Stage Blackpool*, p46.

21. Band says that Mecca followed this rejection by buying a Blackpool site and building a Locarno ballroom which then competed with the Tower Co.'s ballrooms.

22. Band (2005), p46.

23. Band (2005), p23.

24. British Motor Corporation – the motor manufacturing group, now defunct, built up by Lord Nuffield from his Morris motor company, and eventually owning Austin, Morris, MG, Wolseley, Riley, Rover, Land Rover, Daimler and Jaguar brands, before being merged with Leyland Motors and then eventually broken up.

25. Band (2005), p46.

26. If a listed company holds quoted investments, these are now restated every year to current value, so value changes over time are recorded systematically. In the 1960s companies could hold assets at cost as long as any significant diminution in value was seen as temporary. Latent gains and losses were not revealed.

27. Band (2005), pp53–62.

28. Interview with the author, 1 July 2015

11

1. Giving rise to the title of his assisted autobiography 'East End, West End' which has been an invaluable resource.

2. Bernard Delfont & Barry Turner (1990) *East End, West End*, Macmillan, London.

3. For example, when researching this book I bought a record of Reg Dixon playing the Wurlitzer at the Tower Ballroom – recorded, of course, by EMI.

4. Delfont and Turner, p174.

5. Interview with author, 1 July 2015

6. Bank of Credit and Commerce International (BCCI) which went into liquidation in the 1990s is an example of the risks involved.

7. These showed a loss before taxation of £187,000, suggesting that the operating costs from November 1967 to June 1968 were well in excess of revenues ahead of the main July/August peak earning period of the season.

8. A more famous example of this is Apple v. IBM. Apple refused in the 1980s (and still does) to allow other companies to use its computer software, whereas IBM allowed anybody to use the MS-DOS operating system developed for it by Microsoft. As a consequence Apple nearly disappeared in the 1990s, only being rescued by the iPod, followed by the iPhone, followed by the iPad, whereas every other laptop or desktop uses a Microsoft system.

9. Barry Band (2005), *The Main Stage*, Blackpool, p64.

10. Oddly that was also the year that Companies House de-registered the Blackpool Tower Co. (whose name had been changed to EMI (Blackpool) Ltd.). There is no particular practical significance to this – the assets had presumably been absorbed into other group companies – even if it has symbolic significance.

11. Barry Band (2005) includes in its current version an updated last chapter that deals with the Hemmings years and sale to Blackpool Council.

12. This was made up of £10 million from Blackpool Council, £14 million from the Northwest European Regional Development Fund, £7.9 million from the North West Development Agency and £7 million from the Homes and Communities Agency.

ABOUT THE AUTHOR

Peter Walton is a researcher and journalist. He worked as an adminstrative and financial manager for a number of years before turning to journalism and research. He has a doctorate from the London School of Economics and is an emeritus professor at the Open University Business School. His business career included working for EMI at its show business production subsidiary The Grade Organisation, and he subsequently worked for the Isle of Man casino, hotel and entertainment group, where he also managed a small cinema chain. He later provided administrative support to an independent producer with summer shows at Blackpool North Pier, as well as Torquay and Margate.

In his academic career, aside from the Open University, he taught at ESSEC Business School, Paris, and the University of Geneva. In addition, he has taught at Newcastle University and Middlesex University. He has edited academic journals and professional publications and has written many books and articles.

Also Available from Amberley Publishing

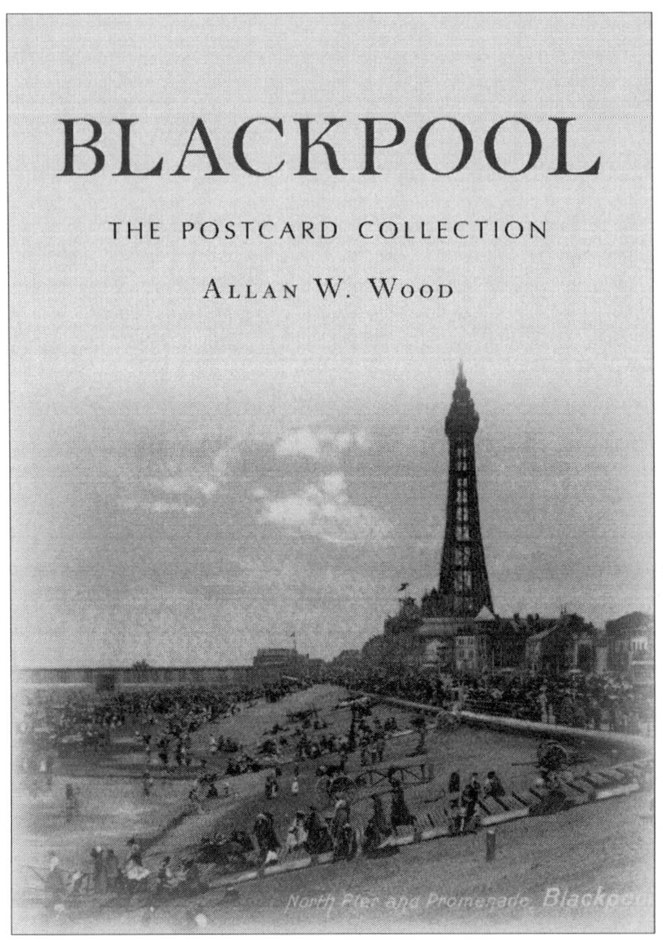

A wonderful selection of postcards depicting the history of
Blackpool, for both citizen and tourist.

Paperback
180 illustrations
96 pages
978-1-4456-4490-5

Available from all good bookshops or to order direct
please call **01453-847-800**
www.amberley-books.com

Also Available from Amberley Publishing

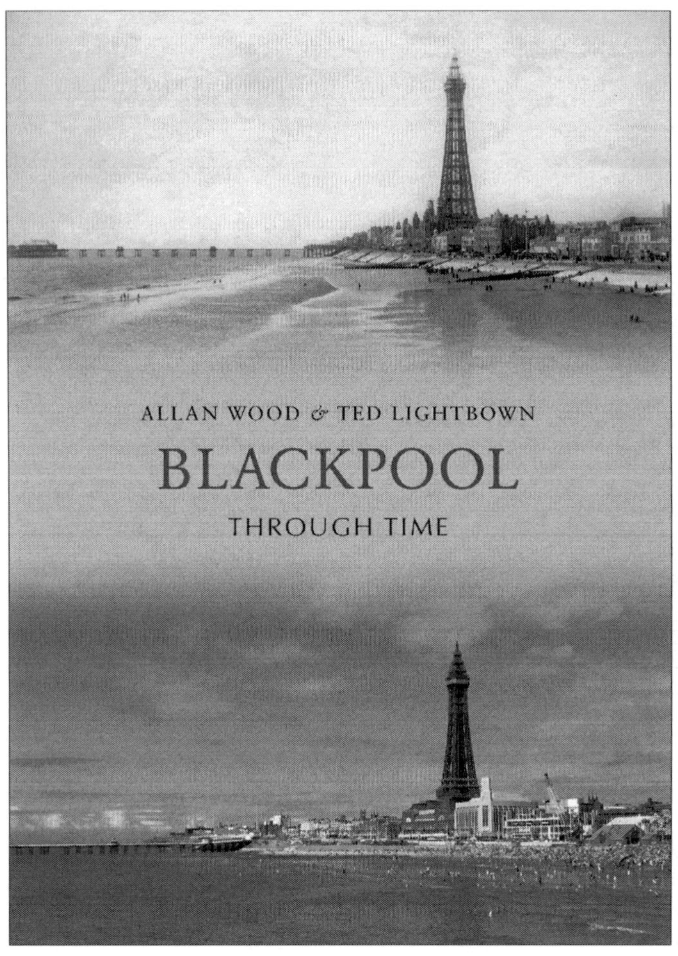

This fascinating selection of photographs traces some of the many ways in which Blackpool has changed and developed over the last century.

Paperback
180 illustrations
96 pages
978-1-8486-8662-5

Available 2014 from all good bookshops or to order direct please call **01453-847-800**
www.amberley-books.com

Printed and bound by CPI Group (UK) Ltd, Croydon, CR0 4YY

26/05/2026

02118210-0004